QATAR

Tamra Orr

 **Marshall Cavendish**
Benchmark

New York

PICTURE CREDITS
Cover photo: © epa/CORBIS
AFP: 115 • age fotostock: Juan Jose Pascual: 7 • alt.TYPE/reuters: 32, 34, 94, 95, 110, 111, 113, 117 •Audrius Tomonis: 135 • besstock: 9, 16, 17, 23, 27, 33, 39, 44, 59, 62, 86, 114, 116 • Chris Mattison: 52 • Chris Mellor/ Lonely Planet Images: 20, 31, 42 • Christine Osborne/Lonely Planet Images: 5, 38 • Christine Pemberton/Hutchison: 46 • Corbis: 25, 45, 54, 71, 73, 99, 100, 102 • James Davis Worldwide: 77 • Mark Daffey/ Lonely Planet Images: 6, 43, 48 • National Geographic Image Collection: 61, 75, 80, 93 • Paul Seheult/Eye Ubiquitous: 125 • photolibrary: 1, 3, 4, 6, 11, 12, 15, 26, 40, 55, 57, 58, 60, 64, 65, 66, 67, 68, 70, 82, 83, 85, 87, 103, 107, 108, 124, 126, 127, 128, 129, 130 • Robin Constable/Hutchison: 24 • Time & Life Pictures/Getty Images: 19 • Tropix.co.uk/ Dominic Jenkin: 78, 101, 109, 120, 121, 122

PRECEDING PAGE
Children riding a donkey through a souq.

Publisher (U.S.): Michelle Bisson
Editors: Christine Florie, Stephanie Pee Cui Zhen, Johann Abang Kassim
Copyreader: Mindy Hicks
Designers: Richard Lee, Rachel Chen Choon Jet
Cover Picture Researcher: Connie Gardner
Picture researchers: Thomas Khoo, Joshua Ang

Marshall Cavendish Benchmark
99 White Plains Road
Tarrytown, NY 10591
www.marshallcavendish.us

All Internet addresses were correct and accurate at the time of printing.

Library of Congress Cataloging-in-Publication Data
Orr, Tamra.
 Qatar / by Tamra Orr. — 1st ed.
  p. cm — (Cultures of the world)
 Summary: "Provides comprehensive information on the geography, history, governmental structure, economy, cultural diversity, peoples, religion, and culture of Qatar"—Provided by publisher.
 Includes bibliographical references and index.
 ISBN-13: 978-0-7614-2566-3
 1. Qatar—Juvenile literature. I. Title. II. Series.

DS247.Q3O77 2008
953.63—dc22   2006033626

Printed in China
7 6 5 4 3 2 1

CONTENTS

A Qatari man enjoys a
quiet moment.

Carpets on sale at a market in Doha.

INTRODUCTION

LEARNING ABOUT THE country of Qatar is a little bit like reading a fairy tale. Qatar found wealth and success through the seemingly unlimited beautiful underwater treasure of pearls. When unexpected events drained that source of revenue, the county found itself poor once again. People struggled to survive in this dry, hot land. Little did they know that the solution to all of their problems was lying deep beneath their feet.

When oil and natural gas were finally discovered in Qatar, poverty and unemployment became a thing of the past. From being one of the poorest countries in the world, it quickly became one of the richest and has remained so ever since.

Although Qatar is still a very young nation, it is resting on the foundations of more than 6,000 years of rich history. While it once was just another piece of land sticking out like a thumb off Saudi Arabia, Qatar has since developed into a modern, exciting, affluent, and desirable place to live, work, and visit. Its lush land, welcoming locales, and business opportunities beckon to many.

GEOGRAPHY

QATAR IS A SMALL country that juts into the Persian Gulf like a stubby thumb. At 4,416 square miles (11,437 sq km), it is slightly smaller than Connecticut. A visitor can drive the entire perimeter in less than 24 hours.

Qatar is part of the multination Middle East or Sharq al Awsat, as the Qatari, or people of Qatar, call it. This 4.6 million square mile (7.4 million sq km) area commonly includes Afghanistan, Egypt, Iran, Iraq, Israel, Jordan, Kuwait, Lebanon, Libya, Oman, Saudi Arabia, Sudan, Syria, Turkey, Yemen, the United Arab Emirates, and the tiny island nation of Bahrain.

Above: **The coastline of Qatar.**

Opposite: **Qatar's Khor Al Udeid Sea provides a refreshing backdrop to the country's desert interior.**

Surrounded on three sides by water, Qatar is a peninsula at a mere 37 miles (60 km) long. Its only land border is with Saudi Arabia in the south. The small islands off the peninsula used to be one large land mass with Qatar, but the passage of millions of years and the endless power of strong winds eventually separated them. Most of these islands are not technically part of Qatar. They are either independent nations or part of other countries like Bahrain. Qatar does have sovereignty, or control, over the islands of Zubarah, Janan Island, and Fasht al Dibal. In recent years, Qatar fought with Bahrain for ownership of Hawar Island in the west, but in a 2001 ruling the International Court of Justice decided that it belonged to Bahrain.

LIVING ON THE EDGE

The geographical design of Qatar is quite unusual. The interior of the country is too dry and rocky for most people to live. Almost all of its cities are located along the coast. The majority of Qatar is just slightly above sea level, so it is quite flat. The highest point in the entire country is Qurayn Abu al-Bawl, a modest hill of 338 feet (103 m). The only other elevation is found in the sand dunes located along the shorelines.

The interior of Qatar is made up of mainly limestone deposits and clay, with lots of sandstone at the surface. It is scrubby with huge patches of gravel and rocks. Although the land is surrounded by ocean, the interior contains no rivers, lakes, or springs of any kind. This means there is a serious lack of fresh drinking water for people and animals. There are 350 miles (563 km) of coast, all made up of white and golden sands that the wind molds into ever-changing shapes. As the sun rises and sets each day, the shades of light color the dunes into endless hues.

LIFE IN THE CITY

There are only about a dozen cities in Qatar. The capital is Doha, home to 612,707 people in the metropolitan area and 339,847 in the city. More than half of the population of the whole country lives in or around Doha.

THE INLAND SEA

At the southeast tip of Qatar is Khor Al-Udeid, or the Inland Sea. It is a beautiful 12-mile (19-km) channel of water created by the Persian Gulf. It cuts into the land to form a shallow lake. On one side are the pink cliffs of Saudi Arabia. On the other are the stark white dunes of Qatar. Although it is definitely one of the most popular spots in the country for Qataris and tourists alike, there are no resorts or hotels there. To keep this spot pristine and beautiful, people must either be driven or boated in, and overnight guests have to stay in tents on the sand. Currently Qatar is trying to have the spot listed as a UNESCO World Heritage Site.

Doha has been the nation's capital since the 1800s, when the ruling family moved from Zubara. It is a beautiful city, recently ranked as the second-best city in which to do business in Arabia, according to *Gulf Business Magazine*. Over the past few decades, the city has transformed itself into a modern place with a changing cityscape and growing skyline. It features a few green parks—a rare sight in this hot, dry place. It has the country's largest port for shipping petroleum. A number of investors have shown a great deal of economic interest in Doha. Tourists spend time in this city enjoying its sports facilities, National Museum, National Theater, and zoo. In addition, Education City, a region dedicated to education and research, is also located there. The Losail International Circuit in Doha is home to an international motorcycling grand prix. The 4.5-mile (7.2-km), crescent-shaped Corniche is in Doha and is a favorite spot for picnickers, joggers, bicyclists, and families out for a casual stroll. In a land of little water, the Corniche's landscaped gardens and greenery are a welcome sight.

Qatar's other cities are much smaller than Doha. Al Rayyan is a suburb of Doha with a rapidly growing population. Its population is already over 200,000. South of Doha is al Wakrah, a fishing

port with more than 30,000 people. It features the al Wakrah Museum which is housed inside an old fort. Mesaieed, formerly known as Umm Said, is an industrial center of more than 12,000 people. It contains both commercial and oil exporting ports and is the site for many of the country's oil refineries.

Near the center of the west coast is Dukhan with a population of 6,400 people. It features beaches and limestone formations. It is also the center for the country's oil and natural gas industries. Al Khor, on the northeast coast is a fishing village of more than 30,000 people. It is expected to grow quickly since it is closely located to the North Field gas industry complex.

Ruwais is on the northern tip of the peninsula. Here visitors can see what traditional Bedouin lifestyle is like as it slowly merges with the ways of the modern world.

A HOT, ARID CLIMATE

In Qatar there is little need for coats or gloves. The weather is almost always hot and dry, and the sun shines virtually every single day. The

COVER YOUR EYES

Sandstorms are not uncommon in Qatar but that does not make them any easier to handle. They occur, without much warning, when convection currents, or winds created by intense heating of the ground, rise up and create a change in the air pressure and temperature. Cooler winds rush in and create a wind that blasts the sand off the tops and sides of the dunes. Dense clouds of brown sand fill the sky like smoke and blot out the sun. Blowing sand can make it impossible to see more than a few feet ahead and cause roads and houses to temporarily disappear. As the wind roars by, people rush to cover their eyes, ears, and noses, and run for shelter.

winter season runs from November to April with average daily temperatures rarely dipping below the mid-60°Fs (16–21°C). Winter brings the only rain, usually less than 5 inches (12 cm) per year. Typically it comes all at once, in violent rainstorms. Southern winds called *gaws* arrive during these months.

May through October is considered summer in Qatar, and the temperatures have been known to reach an amazing 120°F (49°C). Humidity is high, thanks to the gulf moisture and dry northern winds, called *shamal* (Shah-MAHL) blowing hard, often bringing blinding sandstorms in the process.

The creosote bush is a hardy desert plant that is a common sight in the deserts of Qatar.

THE FLORA AND THE FAUNA

With high temperatures and little rain, Qatar does not support much diversity in terms of its animals and plants. Living with limited water and food and intense heat is not easy. Flora and fauna must adapt to harsh conditions and a severe lack of food and water.

Most of the plants in Qatar grow low to the ground and have little to no leaves so they need less rain to survive. Shrubs, sage brush, and creosote are common. Succulents, or plants that can retain water in their leaves, also survive, as well as those with very deep roots. Some plants go to seed and lie dormant, just waiting for those special moments when the rain pours down and wakes them up. The entire landscape changes for the 72 hours after such a downpour. It explodes into bright colors as, for just a brief time, flowers and plants have a chance to soak up each drop of rain and bloom.

The desert dwelling jerboa is well adapted to life in the desert.

Despite the heat and drought, a number of fascinating animals live in Qatar. Many of them are light colored to help them cope with the constant heat of the sun. A number of them also have very large ears to help deflect the high temperatures. The jerboa is a desert-living rodent that can leap up to 10 feet (3 m) at a time. Similar to a kangaroo mouse, it has large ears and eyes and gets most of its moisture from morning dew and plants.

Some animals burrow deeply into the sand to keep cool, while others have special protection around their eyes, ears, and noses to keep out the blowing sand. A great many mammals, like foxes, hares, and wild cats, are nocturnal and hunt at night when the temperatures drop.

Another type of wildlife found in Qatar are insects, such as grasshoppers, crickets, and scorpions. The scorpions, cousins to spiders and ticks, are venomous. They grow as big as five inches (12 cm) long and have narrow bodies, eight legs, and two pinching claws that are able to sense airborne

AN ENDANGERED MASCOT

Once nearly extinct, the Arabian oryx is now the national animal of Qatar. It is such an important symbol of the country that it was the mascot for the 2006 Asian Games hosted there, as well as the icon on the side of the Qatar Airways planes.

The oryx is an antelope that weighs between 140 and 170 pounds (63 and 77 kg). Its body is mostly white with black legs and tail, plus a thick black stripe going up the neck. On top of its head sit two long, black horns that it uses to protect itself. These horns can reach at least 20 inches (50 cm) long! Some people believe that these horns were the original inspiration for the mythical unicorn.

In 1959 there were less than 100 of these animals left in the world. In 1972 the last wild oryx was shot and killed. Different locations throughout the region began raising the oryx in captivity. In 1982 the animals were reintroduced into the wild and by 2003 almost 900 of them were found throughout the area. Now there are almost 1,000. They are still on the endangered list but are making a recovery. To make sure they thrive and grow, the oryx live on protected farms like the one found in Shahaniya. There they graze on vegetation, including seedpods, tubers, roots, and fruit. They can go weeks or even months without water, an important survival technique in a land with limited amounts of the life-giving liquid.

For reasons no one quite understands, the oryx is able to detect rainfall from great distances. It somehow knows where the rain has fallen and if it is living in the wild, it will make its way there in anticipation of the precious greenery that will spring up for a few days.

vibrations. Their tails are segmented and curve up and forward over their bodies. At the end of their tail is a stinger, or telson, filled with poison. During the day, the scorpions hide under rocks but during the night, they come out to prey on spiders and insects. They kill their prey with their lethal sting. Some are even able to capture small lizards and mice. Other insects flying around Qatar include butterflies, moths, dragonflies, beetles, bees, wasps, and mantises. Some of the spiders grow as large as 4.5 inches (11 cm) across.

Reptiles, such as snakes and lizards, are frequently seen in Qatar. Geckos run across the sand, while skinks are able to release their tails when threatened and trying to escape. The broken part continues to wiggle, distracting the predator while the snakelike lizard gets away. Later a new tail will grow out to replace it. Spiny-tailed lizards have sharp claws and although harmless, they are often a tasty treat for some desert dwellers. Snakes are found on the land and in the sea. The horned

KEEPING CREATURES SAFE

In mid-2006 the Supreme Council for Environment and Natural Resources stated that it was beginning a new program for the rare and endangered animal species of Qatar. To protect the animals from being infected by viruses, contagious diseases, or potential epidemics, the organization began immunizing animals in nature reserves and on local farms.

An official at the Ministry of Municipal Affairs and Agriculture told local reporters that "it is a preventative measure that we have decided to take in the wake of deadly viruses such as bird flu, which is filling samples of birds across Asia. . . . The main purpose of the scheme is to save animals that live in our region and [are] already endangered from becoming extinct due to fatal diseases."

viper, is a desert dwelling snake, known to slide down sand dunes in a side-winding position. It makes a distinctive long S-shape in the sand where only two points of its body touch the ground.

Other Qatari creatures can be found in its skies and its ocean. Migrating birds often come through the area in the spring and fall. These include pink flamingos, colorful parakeets, and dark cormorants as well as gulls, ducks, and sparrows.

The sea is also full of life. Four species of dolphins can be found, along with sea snakes, jellyfish, dragon fish, and stonefish. Stonefish are vertebrates with large heads and spiny fins. These fins contain poison with venom strong enough to kill a person who steps on them in shallow waters. Thousands of dugongs live in these waters. They are related to the manatee and reach an average of 9 feet (274 cm) in length. They live on sea grass and are sometimes known as sea cows because they are placid as they move through the water.

The horned viper is so named because of the two horns that protrude from above its eyes.

HISTORY

THE NATION OF QATAR is a new one but its history reaches back thousands of years. Historians believe it was settled as long ago as the Stone Age. A recent discovery in the western part of the country revealed that hunters and fishermen had been there during the Neolithic period. In Shagra, an area in the southeast, a site was found dating back to the sixth millennium B.C. Other discoveries have proven that many different people were living in this region. Some were just passing through the area and decided to stay. They battled each other for the best oyster beds and competed to see who could find the most pearls in the sea. Excavations in Al-khor, Bir Zekrit, and Ras Abaruk have found pottery, flint tools, and ceramic vessels that tie Qatar directly to the al-Ubaid civilization, along the Tigris and Euphrates rivers in Mesopotamia.

During the third to seventh century Qatar played a large part in the trading between the West and the East, supplying cargo ships with purple dye and precious pearls. In the seventh century, however, life began to change as Islam arrived via ships full of Muslim troops traveling across the gulf to conquer Persia (now Iran). When the Qatari were invited to accept Islam as their official religion in A.D. 630, the ruler of the region, Al-Mundhir ibn Sawa al-Tamimi,

Above: **The ruins of a mosque in Qatar.**

Opposite: **The fort of al-Zubara is a symbol of Qatar's turbulent past.**

17

agreed, and all persons living in Qatar became Muslims. Most of them made their living fishing and diving for pearls.

By the mid-1200s Qatar was becoming known as a center for camel and horse breeding, as well as for its pearl industry. The demand for pearls continued to grow from as far away as China. As a result, settlements of small stone houses began to develop on the northern coasts.

UNDER PORTUGUESE RULE

At the beginning of the 16th century, Qatar, along with the rest of the western Persian Gulf, fell under the control of the Portuguese. The Portuguese focused on establishing forts on the southern coastline and creating a commercial empire in the area, exporting gold, silver, silks, cloves, amber, horses, and, of course, the production of pearls.

ROCK ART

Scattered around the eastern and far northwestern coasts of Qatar are a number of rock-carving sites that provide a glimpse into its prehistory. All of them feature some formation of cup marks. Many of them have double rows of cup marks, which archaeologists believe were used to play the ancient game of mancala. This game-board rock art still remains something of a mystery, however, because there are so many of them (333) and some are in locations where it would be impossible to actually sit and play a game.

Other carvings found on rocks in Qatar depict boats, including anchors and oars. These were most likely used to illustrate the art of pearling and fishing.

They remained in power until the mid-18th century when the al-Khalifa and al-Jalahima clans migrated from Kuwait to Qatar. By 1783 these clans had also captured Bahrain and made it their capital. They helped establish important and successful fishing ports in the area. Soon these areas were major stopping points for ships on their trade routes. Most of the people in Qatar lived along the coast, but a few Bedouins were found in the interior. They raised cattle and other animals and lived simple, quiet lives.

The control of al-Khalifa was challenged when the al-Thani clan came to the area from the Najd region of central Arabia and battled for

The exterior of Fort Doha. Qatari warriors built forts like this to protect their land and interests.

British agent Colonel Lewis Pelly was instrumental in negotiating for peace within the different warring groups.

control. Great Britain eventually got involved in the battle, as it had been involved with Qatar ever since coming to the area to stop the Portuguese from charging fees to ships sailing into their ports. The conflict between Great Britain and Portugal over the waterways had been going on for 200 years, which finally, Britain won.

Rahmah ibn Jabir, a transitory Sheikh from the al-Jalahima clan, was eager to make an alliance with anyone who was against the al-Khalifa clan. He found support from the Wahhabis, a group of conservative Muslims who came to the area to spread a much stricter form of Islam than was already being practiced. The two joined forces, and by 1809 had total control of the country. The al-Thani group also embraced this new style of religion and soon, they became the dominant clan. The Wahhabis turned their backs on their former ally, Rahmah ibn Jabir and ousted him in 1816. The al-Khalifas, who had moved to Bahrain but still had considerable influence over Qatar, did not like this turn of events, and in 1867 they attacked Qatar in an attempt to wrest control back. They looted the cities and created chaos. This time Britain intervened and supported the al-Thani group. British agent Colonel Lewis Pelly began negotiating for peace with Sheikh Muhammad ibn al-Thani. Finally, in 1867, the Qataris agreed to a peace treaty that stated Britain would protect the Qatar peninsula. It was the first time in the country's history that it was seen as independent from neighboring Bahrain.

Under the rule of Qasim ibn Muhammad al-Thani, the sheikh's son, Qatar came under Ottoman control. The Ottomans based themselves in Doha and remained in power for many years. However, they were forced out when they entered World War I on the side of the Germans. Qatar supported Great Britain in the war, and leader Sheikh Abdulla ibn Qasim al-Thani promised that in return for Britain's protection, his country would not deal with any foreign countries without Britain's permission.

AN ECONOMIC SHIFT

In the early 1930s the pearl industry collapsed causing Qatar to lose its major source of income. It was not long before poverty, food shortages, and disease became common. After centuries of people coming to the area, they began to leave in hopes of finding work, money, and

DANGEROUS SEAS

During the feud between Rahmah ibn Jabir and the al-Khalifa, it was more dangerous than usual to be out at sea. Rahmah ibn Jabir was in control of much of Qatar and he did not want the interference of others. He and his followers acted as pirates, boarding ships to steal their cargo and killing the passengers, especially if they were from the al-Khalifa clan. Jabir was soon known as the leading pirate of an area that became known as the Pirate Coast. He died on his ship during a battle with yet another al-Khalifa ship. He was lighting the gunpowder keg with the help of his young son when he died.

a better chance for survival elsewhere. For almost a decade, life in Qatar was very hard. All of that changed in 1930, however, when oil prospectors came to the area and struck oil. The sudden influx of money from eager investors caused Abdulla ibn Qasim problems. His relatives began to ask for more and more of the profit and threatened to overthrow the government if they did not get it. The sheikh turned to Britain for protection and it agreed, in return for a greater amount of control over ruling the nation and its oil.

It took another ten years before the oil industry began to develop. World War II had delayed the process. Britain's presence and money from the exportation of oil brought a great deal of improvement to the country. In 1952 the first school opened. Hospitals improved and roads were built. In 1960 the sheikh's son, Ahmad ibn Ali, took over the country and began giving government jobs and high salaries to members of his family. The people protested and went on strike. Soon they formed the National Unity Front. Some of its leaders were jailed while others were exiled. The emir realized, however, that changes needed to be made and began directing more funds to giving land to the poor. He also invested in the development of other industries, including cement factories and farming.

GREAT BRITAIN DEPARTS

In 1968 Great Britain told the Qatari that within three years, they would be pulling all of their military forces out of the nation, ending their years of protection and control. At first it was assumed that Qatar would join with Bahrain and the United Arab Emirates (Abu Dhabi, Ajman, Dubai, Fujairah, Ras al-Khaimah, Quwain), but that soon changed as the nine countries could not agree on the terms of the union. Qatar

FROM THE EMIR

In a speech to the people of Qatar the night before the constitution was adopted, Emir Sheikh Hamad ibn Khalifa al-Thani *(below)* said,

In the Name of God, the Most Compassionate, The Most Merciful. Citizens, Nations and peoples pass through important and crucial phases in their history. Today, we in Qatar witness a historical stage in the march of our beloved homeland towards progress and the building of the state of law and institutions. Since my accession and shouldering the responsibilities and burdens of rule, my goal and aim has been to realize, what I have vowed to God and to you to do my best for the progress and advancement of our country, and to start with you a new era in which we pursue working with all the strength and capabilities we have, to achieve our noble aim of building a prosperous and stable state based on religion and morals its pillars are science and knowledge and the foundation of its governance is justice and the constitution.

wanted its independence and declared it in September 1971. In 1972, while the emir, Sheikh Ahmad ibn Ali al-Thani, was out of the country hunting in Iran, his cousin Sheikh Khalifa ibn Hamad al-Thani took control of the government in his absence.

It was a positive move for the country. The new emir directed less money toward greedy family members and more toward the development of health care, education, and housing. In 1974, when gas prices began to rise all over the world, Qatar's income skyrocketed. While the emir used much of the money to support free services and other city modernizations, he still focused on following the traditional Wahhabi Muslim lifestyle. He insisted on daily prayers, proper dress, and no alcohol.

MODERN TIMES

As an independent country, Qatar has continued to thrive. The first popular elections were held in 1999, and in 2002 a constitution was drafted. In 2003 it was approved and finally implemented in 2005. It allows for free speech, a free press, and freedom of assembly, but does not permit the formation of political parties. It also states that no changes can be made to it for the first 10 years it is in effect.

During the Gulf War of 1990–91, Qatar supported the United States. In 2002 the United States transferred its military facilities from Saudi Arabia to Qatar. The following year Qatar served as the critical command center for the United States during the invasion of Iraq. Thousands of U.S. troops were based on the peninsula, causing tension with some of its neighbors and even a small amount of dissent among its own people.

Today Qatar continues to support its oil industry, while taking the time to invest in other industries in preparation for the day when the oil eventually runs out. The country continues to grow and becomes more modern with each passing year.

Opposite: **Sheikh Khalifa ibn Hamad al-Thani, the man who changed Qatar for the better, came to power while his predecessor was on vacation.**

Below: **His Royal Highness Hamid bin Khalifa Al-Thani with a foreign delegate.**

GOVERNMENT

BECAUSE QATAR ONLY REACHED its independence in 1971, its government is still developing and changing. Today it is a constitutional monarchy, meaning that it is led by a single ruler who is known as the emir. He is the head of state and since the al-Thani clan is the dominant group on the peninsula, the emir is always a male member of this clan. This means that most of the people in power are related, from brothers and sons to nephews and cousins.

MEET THE EMIR

The emir has absolute power over the people. As of 2007 the emir is His Highness Sheikh Hamad ibn Khalifa al-Thani. He is the seventh member of the al-Thani family to rule Qatar. They have been in power since the mid-1800s. The emir was born in Doha in 1952. After going to school in Qatar, Sheikh Hamad enrolled in Britain's Sandhurst Royal Military Academy and graduated in 1971. From there, he joined the Qatari Armed Forces and a year later, he was promoted all the way to the rank of commander-in-chief of the armed forces.

In 1977 Sheikh Hamad was appointed as minister of defence and heir apparent, the person who is next in line to inherit the position of emir. He became emir in June 1995. His heir apparent is Sheikh Tamim ibn Hamad al-Thani, his fourth son, who was appointed in August 2003. Like his father, he went to Sandhurst. His major focus in Qatar

Above: **His Highness Sheikh Hamad ibnKhalifa al-Thani is Qatar's absolute ruler.**

Opposite: **A government building at the Corniche.**

has been on sports. He is chairman of the Qatar National Olympic Committee, a member of the International Olympic Committee, and the Sports for All Committee, as well as chairman of the Doha Asian Games Organizing Committee.

The emir is in charge of creating and enforcing all the laws of his country. He appoints a cabinet or council of ministers to help him follow the sacred Islamic laws of Sharia. His cabinet includes the prime minister, first deputy prime minister, second deputy prime minister, and the state ministries. They work together with the 35-member Advisory Council. Qatar's prime minister is Sheikh Abdullah ibn Khalifa al-Thani. He too is a graduate from Sandhurst. He was appointed in October 1996.

It is the Advisory Council's responsibility to elect a speaker and deputy speaker by secret ballot. The council is divided up into five permanent

THE SUCCESSION OF QATAR RULERS

Sheikh Muhammad ibn al-Thani	1850–78
Sheikh Qasim ibn Muhammad al-Thani	1878–1913
Sheikh Abdullah ibn Qasim al-Thani	1913–49
Sheikh Ali ibn Abdullah al-Thani	1949–60
Sheikh Ahmad ibn Ali al-Thani	1960–72
Sheikh Khalifa ibn Hamad al-Thani	1972–95
Sheikh Hamad ibn Khalifa al-Thani	1995 to present

Many of the names used sound very similar. *Sheikh* is much the same as saying Mister in the United States. Al-Thani is the last name. Ibn means the son of. Muhammad is commonly used to honor the Islamic prophet.

committees: Legal and Legislative Affairs, Financial and Economic Affairs, Public Services and Utilities, Domestic and Foreign Affairs, and Cultural Affairs and Information. The council debates various political, economic, and administrative issues, as well as social and cultural ideas. Its recommendations go directly to the ministers.

The ministers have a number of jobs that they have to handle. First they have to put together a plan for the development of Qatar, and write the laws that must be put into place for the plan to work. They watch to ensure that the laws are implemented by the courts. The ministers keep an eye on all government departments and supervise relationships with other countries.

Qatar's Ministry of Justice guides the country's legal system. It is entirely based on the teachings of Prophet Muhammad, his practices, and Islamic law. Judges consult the Koran, which they consider to be the word of God or Allah, before making decisions

THE NATIONAL ANTHEM OF QATAR

Swearing by God who erected the sky,
Swearing by God who spread the light,
Qatar will always be free,
Sublimed by the souls of the sinceres,
Proceed thou on the manners of the ascendants,
And advance on Prophet's guidance,
In my heart, Qatar is an epic of glory and dignity,
Qatar is land of the early men,
Who protect us at time of distress,
Doves they can be at times of peace,
Warriors they are at times of sacrifice.

on any case. Under Sharia law, a person is considered innocent until proven guilty. In an Islamic court, if a plantiff is not able to produce eyewitnesses to the supposed crime, he can insist that the defendant take an oath of innocence. Since, under Islamic law, liars or perjurers, automatically go to hell, most people will not take the oath unless they truly believe they are innocent. The judge, or *qadi* (KHA-dee), is in charge of asking questions during the case as there are rarely any lawyers or juries present. Under Islamic law, certain crimes like murder, adultery, or theft, carry harsh penalties while lesser ones, such as incurring debt or using alcohol, have lighter punishments. For non-Muslims, there are secular courts that follow a different set of rules.

The other ministries in the council include the Ministry of Defense, Interior, Foreign Affairs, Finance, Economy and Commerce, Endowments and Islamic Affairs, Municipal Affairs & Agriculture, Civil Service Affairs and Housing, Communications and Transport, Education

GOING ONLINE WITH "QATAR'S ELECTRONIC GATE"

In 2002 the emir decreed that governmental electronic services should be offered to the people of Qatar. Making information electronically accessible would speed up transactions and modernize the processes. Currently, citizens, residents, visitors, and businesses can access visa services, traffic violations services, and water and electricity services, along with three dozen additional options on what is referred to as "Qatar's Electronic Gate." The program has been successful, seeing more than 20,000 transactions per month by the end of 2006.

and Higher Education, Energy, Industry, Electricity, and Water, and Public Health.

Qatar's military is small, made up of approximately 12,000 men in the army, navy, and air force. The military played an important part in supporting U.S. military forces during the invasion of Iraq in 2003. It also has a public security force of approximately 8,000 men.

TRANSITION TO DEMOCRACY

The first free elections were held in 1999 and again in 2003. For this country, free elections were a monumental step toward democracy. While these elections did not affect rulers at the national level, they gave the people a voice at the local level. Women were allowed to be

THE NATIONAL FLAG

The flag of Qatar is striking. It consists of a maroon background with a jagged white stripe on the left. The maroon stands for blood, while the white represents peace. Nine serrated points stand for the nine emirates in the Persian Gulf.

The original flag for the nation was red. A narrow stripe was added in 1860 and then in 1932, the serrated stripe was changed to a wavy one. The red became dark violet and then changed to maroon four years later. The current design was adopted in 1971 and has remained unchanged since then.

candidates and voters, a true step toward gender equality in a country where it has been an ongoing battle. Even the emir's wife, Her Highness Sheikha Mozah Bint Nasser al-Missned, has a political role. She is president of the Supreme Council for Family Affairs. Her deputy is also a woman. Sheikha al-Missned formed this council in 1998. Because the Qatari place a great deal of emphasis on the importance of family, al-Missned wanted a separate organization that would focus on family needs and issues. Preservation of the family unit is a high priority in an Islamic nation. In this manner, al-Missned has helped families by establishing the Social Development Center, which focuses on improving the income of families by providing training in various

Her Highness Sheikha Mozah Bint Nazzer al-Missned (*left*) seen here with the chief of India's Congress Party, Sonia Ghandi, has been a strong advocate of women's and family issues in Qatar.

jobs so that they do not have to rely on charity; supporting women through creating an environment where they can engage in social interaction and participate in public life; encouraging conferences that study women's issues; promoting education through Qatar Foundation's Education City where both genders can attend; establishing organizations that provide help and advice to different social groups as through the Qatar Establishment for Care of the Elderly, the Shafallah Center for Children with Special Needs, the Qatar Establishment for the Protection of Women and Children, the Center for Marriage Counselling and the Youth Rehabilitation Center; leading public awareness campaigns and legislative reform

Qatari children are very important to the nation's growth in the future.

such as the United Nation's "Say Yes for Children," which focuses on the ten most important things Qataris need to do to improve the lives of the nation's children.

Sheikh Hamad has made other changes in directing Qatar closer to democracy. In 1996 he lifted the longtime censorship of the press and the following year, he revised the political structure so that the members of the Qatar Chamber of Commerce and Industry Board of Directors were elected through direct votes.

FOREIGN TIES

Although Qatar has strong ties to the Arab countries that surround it, it has also steadily moved toward democracy and in doing so, has

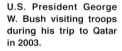
U.S. President George W. Bush visiting troops during his trip to Qatar in 2003.

forged relationships with the United States, along with other Western nations. Qatar has continued to support the United States's presence in Iraq as it works to become a democracy. In 2003 President George W. Bush visited the troops in Qatar and met with the emir. It was the first time a U.S. president had come to this country. In the same year, the emir visited the United States, France, and the United Kingdom. While in Washington, the emir met Secretary of State Colin Powell, Vice President Dick Cheney, and Secretary of Defense Donald Rumsfeld. He delivered a speech to a gathering of business leaders, scholars, and media personalities. To the heads of the leading Arabic and Islamic organizations, he spoke about the strides Qatar was making toward modernization and democracy. He said,

> We believe that the absence of democracy would hinder the drive of development and progress in our Arab and Islamic world. For this reason we in the state of Qatar have planned to exert our best efforts to make the popular participation our policy as a guideline for the state's course of work in all areas of society and for this reason also we have laid down a permanent constitution and conducted a referendum on it; and our people voted in favor of it. . . . Thirst for democracy in our region is what makes the majority of its peoples view with much appreciation the American experience.

Former U.S. secretary of state James Baker said, "The emir is much more than a leader of a country rich in natural resources. He is also a powerful voice for reform and stability in the Gulf and the Middle East."

Another bond exists between the two countries because several large American universities are based in Doha and more are planned in the near future. The emir stresses that this educational link between the countries—not the military one—should be nurtured and broadened.

A COUNTRY OF MEDALS

Qatar awards a number of medals to its highest officers. The Necklace of Independence is the highest honor. It is worn by the emir and is only awarded to present and former kings and heads of state. This necklace is gold and extremely elaborate with pearls, diamonds, and rubies on it. It includes engraving on part of it that reads Religion–Science–Justice–Order–Work–Morals. It also has drawings of the Qatar Oil Company, a boat, a palm tree, a bow and arrow, a college, a sea port, a fertilizer factory, and more.

A WORD FROM THE AMBASSADOR

In the Letter from the Ambassador section of the September 2003 issue of *The Pearl*, the newsletter of the Embassy of the State of Qatar, Bader Al-Dafa wrote,

> Our government, once purely traditional, now has a new constitution which gives every Qatari—be they man or woman, rich or poor—the right to vote and the right to be elected to public office. . . .This transformation started with the idea of liberty, a value which has joined the State of Qatar and the United States in a deepening friendship that has stood the test of difficult times, as Qatar remains a strong ally for the United States in the war on terror. . . By coming together, Qatar and the U.S. have formed not only strategic partnerships in military and trade, but in ideas as well. This partnership is now poised to become an increasingly important force for peace, progress and moderation in the Middle East.

The Necklace of Merit is given to a number of officers, including the heir apparent, prime ministers, among others. It is also gold and engraved with the state emblem of Qatar. The Sash of Independence is given to deputy prime ministers and VIPs, as well as non-Qatari VIPs who help the country or humanity in general. It is made of maroon silk with green and white on the sides, and a gold and pearl medallion in the middle bearing the state emblem. The Sash of Merit is given to ministers, ambassadors, and VIPs. It is made of maroon and white silk with a gold medal in the middle. In addition to the necklaces and sashes, Qatar also gives out five classes of Medals of Merit which can come in the form of a necktie, medal or medallion.

DEFENSE

The Ministry of the Interior is responsible for public security and the maintenance of law and order in Qatar. The police are in charge of keeping order, as well as preventing and investigating crimes. The National Guard is also active in Qatar, often at the borders, in oil fields, and at other important stations throughout Qatar. They also act as backup for the police force if needed.

The police cadets who go on to become officers attend a three-year program at the Police Academy, while National Guard officers go to Kuwaiti Military College to receive specialized training. Occasionally women will be found in departments such as criminal investigation or airport security.

The overall crime rate in Qatar is low with the occasional theft but overall, traffic accidents pose the biggest risk to visitors. They are Qatar's leading cause of death, thank to lots of roundabouts, ongoing construction projects, and high-speed drivers. In the more rural areas, accidents are caused by poor lighting on the road and even the occasional wandering camel.

ECONOMY

AT ONE TIME QATAR'S economy could be summed up in a single word: pearls. When that period of wealth ended, many Qataris wondered what would be next. For almost a decade the answer was hunger, poverty, and disease. When the solution finally came, this time around it was in two words: gas and oil.

TAKE A DEEP BREATH

For centuries Qatar provided other countries with some of the most beautiful natural pearls. Pearls are valued all over the world and had been for hundreds of years, but nowhere perhaps as much as in Arabia. The pearls were loved not only for their beauty, but also because pearls are mentioned in the Koran. When paradise is described, it reads, "The stones are pearls and jacinths [a type of hyacinth]; the fruits of the trees are pearls and emeralds; and each person admitted to the delights of the celestial kingdom is provided with a tent of pearls, jacinths, and emeralds; is crowned with pearls of incomparable lustre, and is attended to by beautiful maidens resembling hidden pearls."

Entire families made a living from diving deep into the ocean in search of the oyster with the perfect treasure inside. It was a difficult and dangerous profession. Divers often had to dive much farther than they wanted to. Some even attached stones to their feet in order to get deeper. They learned to hold their breath for several minutes and wore clips, much like clothespins, on their noses. Divers wore leather

Above: **This fountain in Qatar serves to remind its people of the importance pearls once had in Qatar's economy.**

Opposite: **Doha is a modern city in a modern economy.**

protection on their hands because oyster shells are sharp, and it was a huge risk to try and grab them with bare hands. Sharks and other dangerous creatures were additional risks under the water.

When the divers had all the oysters they could hold in the bags around their necks, they swam to the surface. After emptying their bags onto the boats, they would go back down again, often making 30 or more trips in a day. The people rarely ate or drank anything

INSIDE THE OYSTER

The process of making a pearl has little to do with creating anything beautiful—at least from the oyster's perspective. It is simply trying to protect itself.

An oyster is made up of two parts called valves. They are held together by a ligament that helps open the oyster to let food in. When a foreign substance slips inside and lodges between the shell and the mantle, or the organ responsible for producing the shell, it irritates the mantle. It is a little like a person getting a "splinter."

To make the splinter go away, the pearl begins covering it up in layers with the same material that is used to construct the shell. This ends up being a natural pearl. A number of other countries discovered a way to cultivate pearls by opening the oysters up and making a small cut on the mantle. The oyster reacts the same way to the cut as it does to the foreign substance and ends up making a cultured pearl. Although the two are often considered of equal quality, the natural pearl usually costs more because it is much more rare.

before diving, instead, they waited until the end of the day. After the oysters were opened and any pearls removed, the shells were thrown back into the sea because an old legend stated that during the night the shells would rise to the surface and open up to capture a drop of dew which would turn into a pearl again later.

The pearl industry was reaching its peak around 1930 when the unthinkable happened: the Japanese came up with a way to create cultured pearls. This process made pearls less expensive and much easier to obtain. Qatar's pearl industry collapsed and cost many people their livelihoods.

BENEATH THEIR FEET

Life became difficult in Qatar. Hundreds of people began leaving the peninsula to find jobs in neighboring nations. Food was limited, and poverty was common. Fortunately rescue came in the form of two highly valuable commodities: oil and natural gas.

Oil was first discovered in 1939. It took ten years before production was up and running, because World War II had the attention of the world. Those were difficult years for the Qataris as hunger and lack of work continued to plague their lives. Once oil production was finally underway, the nation changed almost overnight. Money poured into the country and was immediately used to improve homes, open schools and hospitals, build roads, and make life easier for everyone. Qatar was on its way to becoming one of the world's wealthiest countries. Unemployment disappeared and in fact, there was a severe shortage of workers, and soon, people from surrounding countries were moving to Qatar in search of jobs. It would not be long before these foreigners far outnumbered the native Qataris, a situation that still exists today. The majority of the labor force in Qatar comes from other places!

Oil and natural gas production began in western Qatar, particularly in the North Field, the largest natural gas field in the world. By 1964 offshore production had begun in the waters east of the peninsula. The oil and natural gas were transported to the city of Messaieed and from there, exported to Japan, South Korea, India, the UAE, Thailand, Singapore, and the United States by ship. Today Qatar is estimated to have more than 900 trillion cubic feet of natural gas reserves and 16 billion barrels of oil reserves. This makes it the third-largest reserve in the entire world after Russia and Iran.

Natural gas production has proven to be more complicated than oil production because of difficulties in exporting gas. To be truly

CURRENCY FACTS

Until 1959 the type of currency used in Qatar was the Indian rupee. The country briefly used the Gulf rupee, and then the Saudi riyal along with Dubai. Finally, in 1973, when Dubai joined the United Arab Emirates, Qatar began issuing its very own currency.

Today it uses the Qatari riyal, which can be divided into 100 dirhams. Banknotes come in denominations of 1, 5, 10, 50, 100, and 500 riyals, while coins come in denominations of 1, 5, 10, 25, and 50 dirhams. In December 2006, 1 U.S. dollar was worth 3.64 riyals.

economical, the gas has to be converted to liquid form so that it takes up much less space. It is a slow process, however, that requires extremely high pressure and very low temperatures. Continual improvements are being made to the refining, transporting, and exporting processes because natural gas is often thought to be the fuel of the 21st century as it is far less damaging to the environment than burning oil or coal.

Currently petroleum production and exportation provide about 70 percent of the nation's revenue and while it certainly has proven to be the true salvation to Qatar, it is a limited one. Experts predict that by the year 2025, half of Qatar's oil and natural gas supplies will be exhausted. Because of this, in recent years the emir has worked hard to diversify Qatar's sources of revenue. There is a growing emphasis on developing new businesses, such as financial services,

The Mesaieed oil and petrochemical refinery in Qatar.

THE NORTH FIELD

Located off the north shore of the peninsula is the largest natural gas field in the world, the North Field. It was first discovered in 1971. It covers an amazing 2,317 square miles (6,000 square km), almost half of Qatar's total land area. Currently, production from this field alone is 6.6 million tons per year of liquefied natural gas, and with the recent addition of two more trains to transport it, the Qatari people hope that it will reach its new goal of producing 9 million tons per year.

Workers at the degassing station in Dukhan which is the center of Qatar's oil production.

chemicals, and tourism. Cement and fertilizer plants have been built, as well as steel smelters and flour mills. Foreign investors are more than welcome, and business people from all over the world come to Qatar to explore its economic possibilities.

Just like the oil and gas industries, all businesses in Qatar are controlled by the government. Although it is in charge of Qatar's economy, people are allowed to run their own businesses as long as those businesses do not go against the interests of the country itself. Unemployment is almost unheard of since it is the duty of the government to provide a job for anyone who needs one. With everyone working, there is virtually no poverty and in turn, Qatar has an extremely low crime rate.

In 2006 Qatar's hotel industry grew in response to the millions of fans coming for the Asian Games.

OTHER THAN OIL

While oil and gas production make up the main portion of Qatar's income, it is not the only industries in the country. Agriculture accounts for less than 2 percent of the nation's revenue. Since there is so little available water and arable land, it is a challenge to grow strong crops. Many farmers depend on a combination of sewage water and desalinated water to irrigate their crops. They typically grow just enough vegetables, like eggplant, squash, tomatoes, and cereal grains, to feed their own people, while others raise animals. Qatar has approximately 10,000 heads of cattle, 33,000 camels, 140,000 goats, 150,000 sheep, 2.2 million chickens, and 71.42 metric tons of various kinds of seafood.

WELCOME TO QATAR

One economic area that Qatar is very interested in developing is tourism. In 2004 the Qatari saw around 400,000 tourists come through their country to enjoy the sandy beaches and hot weather. By 2010 Qatar hopes to have more than one million tourists stopping by for a vacation.

This goal may happen sooner than later. In December 2006 Doha hosted the Asian Games. Millions of sports fans poured into the little nation. In preparation, Qatar frantically invested in and made fairly massive changes and improvements to its infrastructure. It built four new hotels, extended the airport, constructed sports stadiums, and improved its roads and highways. The 2006 mascot, Orry, was seen everywhere, and the International Airport was covered with signs and posters promoting the games. The Qatar Tourism Authority was formed in 2000 and has remained focused on making its country one of the world's leading destinations for leisure, business, and sport, and so far, it is succeeding.

In addition to preparing for the Asian Games, Qatar's United Development Company is also in the midst of building a multibillion-dollar artificially-made island covering 985 acres (329 ha) off its eastern shore. Called the Pearl-Qatar, it is projected to be finished by 2009. According to the developers, this island will be "a unique living and cultural experience that integrates the best of the country's past and present." They plan to have everything from luxurious villas on the beaches to apartments with ocean views and several five-star hotels. When it is completed, it will accomodate 40,000 people. It will be a reclusive retreat similar to the famous French Riveria.

The island will be connected to the mainland by a causeway so that residents have easy access to the rest of the country. It will include three marinas, three primary schools, one secondary school, and a number of shops and restaurants. Planners hope it will attract many visitors and future permanent residents. They state "The Pearl-Qatar will be a destination in its own right—a lavish, secure, and exclusive island retreat in a Riviera-style community."

UTMOST CARE

In a speech to the U.S. Foreign Relations Council, the emir stated that, "We, in the State of Qatar, accord utmost care to economic development, as a top priority and a key instrument to fulfill the cherished aspirations in building up of both the nation and the nationals, in improving the living standards of the people and in preserving our natural resources."

ENVIRONMENT

IN MANY WAYS QATAR seems safe from any environmental problems. It is in a remote location and has a fairly small population. However, it has to deal with its own unique problems.

In 1984 the Supreme Council for the Environment and Natural Resources (SCENR) was created to help the Committee for Environmental Protection keep an eye on various environmental issues. It consists of a deputy president, a number of environmental experts, and a secretary-general. Its biggest concerns are preservation of the natural wildlife; increasing the water supply; and limiting air, water, and land pollution. These concerns fit in well with Islamic doctrine, which tells its followers that nature is a divine gift, and humanity is charged to protect it.

Opposite: **Wild camels in the sand dunes of the empty quarter.**

THE SCENR RULES

While the SCENR has many duties, some of the most important ones include:
- prohibiting trading in or dealing with all endangered wildlife, dead or alive;
- prohibiting hunting of wild birds or animals in all natural sanctuaries, islands, sites, and villages;
- establishing set hunting seasons and penalties for any violations;
- monitoring to ensure that hunters do not damage gardens or farms of plant covers, nor use explosives;
- ensuring that hunters do not interfere or tamper with the life of wild birds, marine turtles, baby animals, wild eggs, and nests unless for scientific research that has been pre-approved by SCENR;
- restricting hazardous waste materials from entering the country as it does not have the facilities to deal with them. No waste materials are to be buried in any Qatari territory without the SCENR's approval.

WATER DISTILLATION IN QATAR

The biggest problem facing the people of Qatar is the severe lack of water. There are no aquifers (an underground bed of porous rock or sediment that yields water) to depend on. There are no sources of fresh water like ponds, rivers, or lakes. The only source of water found in Qatar is the ocean. Obviously it is not helpful because it is far too salty to be used on plants or given to people or animals. The only way to use it is to find a way to get the salt out of it. This is done through a process called desalination. To do this, Qatar officials built desalination plants.

To remove the salt, ocean water is heated in one container until the water evaporates. The salt is left behind. The salt-free steam is caught in another container and cooled off until it changes back to being water. Qatar's desalination plants use this method for getting fresh water but on a much larger and grander scale. Currently Qatar has three plants; a small one is located in Ras Abu Aboud, and two bigger ones are in Ras Abu Fontas. Together they produce about 100 million gallons of water daily.

TACKLING WATER POLLUTION

Pollution is also an issue in Qatar for several reasons. Six to eight million barrels of oil were spilled into the waters during the Persian Gulf War and still affect the nation's oceans today. The oil industry, although bringing wealth and stability to the country, has also had negative effects. It is a constant threat to the water surrounding the offshore fields. In addition the construction of processing plants has pushed the limited number of animals on the peninsula out of their natural habitats. Some of the oil wells also tend to leak or seep, contaminating the ground and water around it and eventually harming plants and animals.

To help remind all of the people of Qatar about the importance of the environment, the SCENR organizes Qatar Environment Day annually. For several days, the people focus on different environmental issues. Past activities have included a march of 2,000 students and adults throughout Doha, led by horses and the Qatari military band, and painting and

An offshore gas platform. Any leaks could have severe consequences on the surrounding marine life.

drawing competitions for children. Food stands and live entertainment lend the day a festive air. Each year more people and organizations get involved and combined, number more than 5,000. At the 2006 celebration, the theme was "Qatar and the Deserts of the World." There were lectures, group discussions, a cleanup campaign, and an exhibition of paintings focused on environmental issues.

In 2004 the New Central Environmental Laboratory was established in Abu Hamoor. It is run by seven Qatari women trained in environmental analysis. They pay close attention to the conditions of coastal waters as well as other pollution problems.

A FLOWER EACH SPRING

Since the late 1990s the emir's wife, Sheikha Mozah Bint Nasser al-Missned, has sponsored a program called "A Flower Each Spring." This program is aimed at bringing people's attention to the importance of taking care of the environment. The sheikha said, "We need to care for our natural environment for it was entrusted to us by God to use with responsibility and respect for the benefit of human kind. If we nurture our environment, it will nurture us."

Each year one Qatari plant is chosen for the people to learn about so that they can better protect it. Thousands of students from government and expatriate schools participate in field trips where they can observe the plant and sometimes even plant more of them. One year the focus was on the peninsula's mangrove forests. The

Opposite: **Qataris are encouraged to learn more about their natural vegetation.**

RASHID THE RECYCLER

The people of Qatar were introduced to the idea of recycling in 2003 by a young, animated Qatari boy. He was the program's mascot named Rashid the Recycler. In a 71-page booklet made out of recycled paper and launched through the Middle East by the United National Educational, Scientific and Cultural Organization (UNESCO), Rashid outlines all the different ways that people can help recycle at school and at home. He tells children all about paper recycling, as well as glass, metal, steel, plastic, and aluminum. "Let's be more aware about the environment and more concerned about our surroundings by focusing on sustainable development," he suggests. As it says in the booklet, "The children of today will be the environmental managers of tomorrow."

Included with the booklet was a CD-ROM, a quiz, and a chance to win an environmental award. The winner was a young Qatari boy named Yousif Tajir Al Sada. He and his teacher traveled to UNESCO's headquarters in France and saw a number of world heritage sites.

A newer version of the booklet is being prepared, this time titled "Rashid & Dana the Recyclers" to reflect the slowly growing awareness of gender balance. Dana is Rashid's sister and together, they will travel to each Arab country to create awareness about various recycling issues. This is vital information for the people of Qatar. Statistics show that only 3 percent of a potential 80 percent of recyclable waste products are actually being recycled.

black mangrove or *al-qurm,* grows along the coasts in several places in Qatar. They keep the coastline strong and protected against the currents of the water. They also shelter a number of species of birds and fish. In recent years these trees have been threatened but, through this program, people were encouraged to plant seedlings and keep the trees safe. There are very few wildlife reserves or national parks in Qatar due to its lack of rain and biological diversity. One spot that does call to people, however, is Al Bida Park, located at the Corniche. It includes something for everyone, including skateboarding ramps and rollerblading paths, ornamental pools and waterways,

Black mangrove forests like this are important to Qatar's ecosystem.

wood bridges, souvenir stalls, an art gallery, and the well-known "pearl man," who always has a beautiful selection of Asian pearls to show off to customers. The park also offers an outdoor theater and a children's playground.

NEW PROJECTS ON THE HORIZON

Recently, as the concern for environmental safety has increased, new projects have developed in Qatar. In late 2006 an uninhabited island

Qataris engaging in outdoor activities on the pathways of the Corniche.

known as Umm Tais, off the northern coast was turned into a nature park. There, visitors are able to see mangrove forests, as well as numerous species of migrating birds, turtles, and other reptiles and fish. The Umm Tais National Park Project aims to be an ecotourism destination, a means to educate the Qatari about the importance of the environment, while protecting the country's natural heritage.

Another project that illustrated the positive effects of recycling was the biodiesel project. To see how well this alternative fuel works, a great deal of cooking oil used in catering for the Asian Games was donated to the Secondary School for Industrial Technology to recycle into biodiesel, an environmentally friendly, biodegradable, nontoxic fuel. To showcase the project, a specially labeled bus transporting the Torch Relay team for the Asian Games was fueled with it.

In addition, an overnight Youth Camp is being set up in the desert, and all participants will get an environmental information package and participate in a number of environmentally-based activities.

THE FALCON CENTER

Falcons are important in Qatar. They are a favorite source of sport and hunting, as well as a respected creature. In Doha the Qatar Falcon Center exists solely to take care of sick and injured falcons. It has three wards where these birds are treated for everything from broken bones and injured wings to dietary problems and foot injuries. The center is closed to the public but occasionally, if the center is not busy, tourists have been allowed to come in and get a quick tour of this hospital that helps falcons.

THE AL SHAQAB STUD

One of the emir's highest priorities for Qatar is returning top-quality Arabian horses to the area. They are used often in desert marathons and other equestrian events. One way to ensure their development is through the creation of special farms where these horses are bred and taken care of. They are exercised and trained in luxurious centers that include treadmills, tracks, and pools. One of these farms is called the Al Shaqab Stud. It is located in the town of Al Rayyan, near the coast of the Arabian Gulf, not far from Doha. It is the site

of one of the most important battles in history—when the Turks were vanquished by Qatari warriors: one of the most important battles in Qatar's history. They base their dedication to these unique horses on the following Islamic poem:

> By the (Steeds)
> That runs, With panting (Breath)
> And Strike sparks of fire,
> And Push home the charge
> In the morning
> And raise the dust in clouds the while
> And penetrate forth with
> Into the midst (of the foe)
> En Masse

The manager of Al Shaqab, Sheikh Hamad ibn Ali al-Thani, said, "Among the most important lesson's [sic] we've learned is this: breeding is heart and eye. The eye needs patience, the heart needs love."

QATARIS

THE QATARIS ARE UNIQUE because they are actually a minority in their own homeland. Although Qatar's population is approximately 885,359, only about 221,000 or 25 percent of the people are from Qatar. They are the descendants of a migratory tribe from the Najd in central Saudi Arabia. The collapse of the pearl industry caused many Qataris to leave Qatar to find work, while the discovery of oil brought foreign workers rushing to fill an almost limitless number of jobs. The population of the peninsula today is 50 times what it was in 1949!

Above: **The growth of the oil industry saw an influx of foreign workers into Qatar looking for employment.**

Opposite: **Qatari children enjoy the pleasures of living in a modern place.**

While Qataris make up about 25 percent of the overall population, Pakistanis and Indians make up 18 percent of ethnic groups. Arabs make up another 40 percent of the ethnic groups, and 10 percent of the people are Iranians. The other ethnic groups are a mix of Palestinians, Lebanese, Omanis, Syrians, Egyptians, East Africans, and Europeans. A small number of Bedouins also pass through from time to time, depending on the season.

Almost all of the people living in Qatar, whether natives or expatriates, live in the outer cities. Half of them are found in the capital city of Doha. Despite the immense mingling of cultures and traditions, all of the ethnic groups get along quite well. Each of them manages to maintain their own individual lifestyle, follow their own separate religious beliefs, eat their favorite cuisine, and wear their own style of clothing.

Bedouin in the desert with their camels.

Bedouins are very family oriented. One of their favorite sayings is, "I against my brothers, I and my brothers against my cousins, I and my brothers and my cousins against the world."

LIFE AS A BEDOUIN

The life of a Bedouin is a nomadic one. These groups have existed for hundreds of years out in the hot desert, a place most try to avoid. Their name means "desert dweller" in Arabic. On the move they follow the grazing needs of their herds, that include camels, horses, sheep, and goats. They do not travel about aimlessly, however. Instead, their destinations depend on a number of factors, such as seasonal change, weather patterns, and the locations of water wells. During the winter, when the only rains come, their animals feast on temporary green carpets of grass and other plants. During the hot, dry summer, most Bedouins and their animals move to the steppe-like areas where some vegetation can still be found. Today Bedouins are found throughout the sandy deserts of most Middle Eastern states. The largest group of Bedouins are found in Northern Saudi Arabia, Western Iraq, and Syria.

To provide shelter, the Bedouin typically use tents. They are easy to put up and take down, as well as simple to repair and transport. Most importantly, these tents protect them against the heat of the sun and the chill of nighttime winds. Many Bedouins use the hair from black Arabian goats to make their tents. They called these shelters *Bait al Shaar,* or the "House of Hair."

Wool that is woven in long strips is used to make the roofs of these dwellings. They are secured to the ground by ropes and poles, much like modern day tents are. Inside the tents, curtains are hung

Bedouins typically live in tents that protect them from the harsh desert conditions and are lightweight and easy to transport when they move.

to create separate rooms for privacy and to set up a room just for receiving visitors.

The Bedouins' daily diet depends on what nature provides. If markets are near where the people travel, a trip is made to replenish supplies. Camel milk is a regular item on their menu, as is tea and coffee. Large meals are served at night, and everyone eats together. Communal platters of food are shared with a half dozen others and often contain a meal of lamb and rice. Dates and vegetables are also common.

Bedouin women keep busy making a variety of handiwork. Camel bags are made out of dyed wood and beads, tassels, and sashes

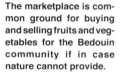

The marketplace is common ground for buying and selling fruits and vegetables for the Bedouin community if in case nature cannot provide.

are then added. Beautiful panels of woven wool hang outside the tents to add color to the brown landscape. Nights are often spent storytelling, singing songs, and reciting poems.

The objects carried and used by today's Bedouins are quite different. Now these include binoculars, sunglasses, and tanks of propane gas. Camels have given way to trucks and automobiles so that when it is time to move, everything is simply loaded onto these vehicles. Even the animals get to ride! Although the Bedouin lifestyle is slowly beginning to fade away as progress and modernization move into their areas, it is still a way of life that some will keep following as long as possible.

QATARI LIFE

The Qatari have seen a surge in the focus on education in their country in the last 50 years. It was not until 1952 that the first primary school was introduced to Qatar. In the same year, four schools were built for boys and one for girls. Although many of the people could not read at that time, they all appreciated storytelling and knew their beloved Koran by heart.

Today the picture is quite different. The last two emirs have placed a huge emphasis on education. Today virtually all elementary-school-aged children attend school for six years and 95 percent of them go on to three years of middle school and three years of secondary school as well. Secondary school offers specialized classes in business training, technical education, religious studies, and teacher training. However, boys and girls still have to attend separate schools. They begin at 7:00 in the morning and end at 1:00 in the afternoon. Literacy for people aged 15 and older is 89 percent. There are also a number of schools

for the children of expatriates. In 1973 the University of Qatar opened in Doha.

The Qatari are hard workers and place great importance on the value of family. Weekends are almost always spent with their children, meals are eaten together daily, and extended family gatherings are common. Hospitality is a strong priority of the Qatari, and friends are invited over for dinner in their homes. Men gather in one room and women are in another.

In Qatar, extended families often live near each other in what is known as tribes. Tribes are further broken down into clans and then to individual households. Marriages are traditionally arranged between tribes rather than with outsiders. In fact anyone wanting to marry an outsider must obtain the permission of the Ministry of the Interior—and it is not always given.

Elderly parents usually live with their children and grandchildren. Although the government has many social services in place to help this older generation, it would be considered shameful if families did not automatically take care of their elders. In the same respect, children are highly honored within Qatari families. Children are welcomed virtually everywhere they go, and it is common to see families enjoying free time together. These values are even included in the Qatari constitution, Article 21: "The family is the basis of society. A Qatari family is founded on ethics, religion, and patriotism. The law shall regulate adequate means to protect the family and support its structure, strengthen its ties, and protect motherhood, childhood and old age."

A Qatari family forms the basis of Qatari society.

LIFESTYLE

LIFE IS MUCH EASIER in Qatar than in many other countries. With unemployment and crime rates low and revenues high, this is not a country of people who must struggle to survive. The government is responsible for providing every family with employment and housing. The Qataris focus on the importance of their religion and their families, as well as preserving the values and morals that makes them who they are.

THE SEPARATION OF THE SEXES

Because Qatar is predominantly an Islamic country, there are a number of rules about keeping men and women separate that are still followed. Although women are definitely making strides in achieving equality, they continue to be treated differently from men. They may be allowed to vote, drive cars, have jobs, and attend universities, but the separation of the genders is a part of daily life. When meeting in public, the two sexes do not shake hands or touch. Even eye contact is relatively limited. Among the same sex, however, touching is common, and it is not

ADVICE FROM THE KORAN

There are a number of statements in the Koran to support the concept of keeping males and females separate. One of them reads, "Tell the believing men to lower their gaze and be modest: that is purer then. Lo! Allah is aware what they do. And tell the believing women to lower their gaze and to be modest, and to display of their adornment only that which is apparent, and to draw their veils over their bosoms."

unusual to see good friends embrace, hold hands, or link arms as they walk. Some will even kiss each other on the cheek or touch their noses together. In school, boys and girls study in separate classrooms, and this continues all the way through college.

Stores, shops, and other public places often set up special hours during the day that are designated as "women and family hours." Some banks even have branches dedicated only to female customers. Businesses such as the post office, the police station, and ticket venues offer "Women-Only" lines. During this time, only women come in, allowing them to shop or do their errands without concerns of dealing with the opposite sex. Even elevators in high rise buildings tend to be gender segregated.

THE UNIVERSITY OF QATAR

A student attending the University of Qatar has six colleges to choose from: the College of Education, Arts and Sciences, Sharia and Islamic Studies, Engineering, Law, and Business and Economics. As the largest and only state-supported university in the country, the University of Qatar is the only local university with a student body so diverse that it represents the entire globe. The student body is commonly made up of students from at least 50 different countries and half a dozen continents. Even the faculty represents diversity, with members from 30 different nationalities on staff. The University of Qatar is chaired by the heir apparent.

The large campus covers three square miles and offers some fascinating opportunities to learn. It has the only marine vessel in the country. It is stocked with state-of-the-art equipment for its ocean-related experiments and studies. The campus also has two planetariums for studying astronomy and space exploration.

The university had 150 students when it originally opened. Today it has more than 9,000 students, three-quarters of whom are women. Classes are gender-segregated, which means that men and women do not sit in the same rooms at the same time.

IN THE HOME

Hospitality and good manners are both extremely important to the Qatari. They welcome guests in their homes at all times and traditionally cook extra food and set an extra place setting at the table in preparation of unexpected visitors. Guests are always offered a drink and a sweet treat. Many homes have a room called the *majlis* where only men meet in. They sit and talk while sharing a cup of hot tea or strong coffee, while the women gather in another room.

Etiquette is important at all times. The left hand is never used for eating or shaking hands. The soles of the feet are never exposed. In the main rooms, chairs are often placed against the wall so that no one who stops by needs to worry about turning his or her back on another person—a sign of rudeness in this culture. When entering another's home or office, or even if just walking into a crowded elevator, the Qatari greet others by saying *"As Salam Alaikom"* or "Peace be upon you." Others respond with *"Wa alaikom as Sala"* or "And peace be with you."

Both middle- and upper-class families almost always employ outside help in their homes. Nannies, gardeners, maids, and cooks are commonplace. The Qatari home often reflects wealth in its architecture and is decorated ornately with porches, balconies, arched windows, and courtyards. Despite this display of modern wealth, most homes also reflect years of tradition by including at least one room decorated traditionally with embroidered silks and floor cushions. Homes commonly smell of incense, which is burned in most rooms, in clay pots.

GETTING MARRIED

Because of the strong Islamic influence in Qatar, wedding ceremonies are quite different from other countries. They are both family and business matters. Many marriages are still arranged by either the couple's mother or the father. Potential grooms are virtually always selected from another family's extended family or tribe. Grooms are often not chosen for their appearance or interest in a young woman, but because it would be a wise business decision to unite the two families. While marriage to someone from the clan is not forbidden,

THE ROLE OF INCENSE

One of the primary aromas floating about Qatar's small businesses and individual homes is that of incense, typically sandalwood or frankincense (*below*). Incense has been used for centuries, often for religious reasons. It is not surprising that it is used in Qatar where the country's name is the Hebrew root word meaning "to make sacrificial smoke."

it is certainly not encouraged. The bride-to-be is often quite young, sometimes as young as 14 or 15 years old. In the past, brides were younger but now there is more of an emphasis on allowing young women to finish high school first.

A young woman is allowed to spend time with her intended only under the watchful eyes of adult chaperones. The tradition of giving the bride's family a bridal dowry, or *mahr*, continues, although it happens less than it used to.

Wedding ceremonies commonly last for days and there are separate ones for the bride and groom. For many women, a favorite wedding

Some young people in Qatar need a little help finding that special someone to marry. In this situation the families call upon the khatiba, *an experienced, older woman who knows the local families very well. For a fee, she will locate a bride for a young man's family.*

ritual is "henna night." A henna artist from a local beauty salon comes to the house and adorns the bride and her sisters's and friends's arms, feet, hands, and ankles with intricate patterns made of henna. This is a dye made from the green leaves of a henna plant, along with ingredients like tea, coffee, or cloves. This henna "tattoo" is temporary and fades away after a few weeks. The women often sing and dance during the ceremony.

Finally, on the wedding night, the bridal couple are allowed to be in the same room together when the groom is taken to the bride's reception to sit with her and her guests.

While some modern couples choose to have a wedding at one of the luxury hotels in Qatar, a number still traditionally have them in open air. Tents are set up for the women and men and the surrounding grounds are covered with carpet and hundreds of chairs. Hanging lights lend a festive air. Since weddings are important celebrations, many people come to enjoy the singing and dancing.

Many Qatari women opt to wear the white and ivory wedding dresses of the Western world, although some still wear the traditional *al-Kazz,* or silk, handmade dress. Men typically wear a uniform known as a *bisht,* a long woolen cloak often covered in fancy and unique patterns.

The wedding night is spent at the home of the groom's parents in a special room called the *al-khalla.* The bride comes into the room carried on a carpet by her brothers or other male relatives. Before leaving the room the next morning, the groom places a piece of gold or some bank notes under the pillow to express his love and pleasure for his new wife. The couple usually stays for a week before moving into their new home.

QATARI CLOTHING

In such a hot land, traditional clothing usually centers more on keeping cool and comfortable than anything else. In the summer, men typically wear loose-fitting cotton cloaks known as *dishdashas* (dish-DAH-shahs), or robes, which are worn over a floor length white shirt and pants. A number of men, as part of their religious beliefs, also wear a *gutra,* or head covering. It is usually long and white, or red and white, and secured in place with four *uqal,* or black, tasseled cords that are braided. Sandals are traditionally worn on the feet.

Women, on the other hand, are often clad in loose, concealing silk black dresses known as *abayahs* and a black scarf on their heads called a *shayla* (SHAY-la). The contrast between the men's white clothing and the women's black clothing is visually startling and distinctive. Some women wear *burkhas* (BUHR-kahs), veils, or masks that cover the lower half of their faces and sometimes their hair. Girls commonly start wearing them about age seven.

GOING TO MARKET

Although much of Qatar is modernizing as quickly as possible, there is one area that remains true to tradition, and that is the *souqs* (SOOKS), or traditional markets. In Doha, one can find rows and rows of these shops selling everything from fragrant Arabian spices (*right*) and perfumes, beautiful tapestry rugs and fabrics, to valuable pearls and gold.

Wandering through the *souqs* is a little like taking a trip through a large and fascinating maze. The Souq Waqif is located in the middle of the city and is one of the oldest markets in existence. Lines of buyers and tourists weave their way from stall to stall looking for cooking utensils, clothing, jewelry, and even weapons. Handmade crafts give visitors candid glimpses into the culture and the skills found in local craftsmen. *Souqs* are able to compete with the large department stores and malls due to their local flavor and authenticity, and its old-fashioned flavor that draws people to keep on buying.

Others wear veils that cover all of the face, except for the eyes, nose, and mouth. Much of this tradition is based on the Koran saying, "O Prophet! Tell thy wives and the daughters, and the women of the believers to draw their cloaks round them [when they go aboard]. That will be better, so that they may be recognised and not annoyed." Non-Muslim women wear clothing that reflects a modern Western style of dress.

During special events, such as weddings or local festivals, both men and women will put on their more elaborate clothing. It is often the same style as what is normally worn, only enhanced with gold and silver embroidery. Women often add a colorful head scarf to their outfits. It is also not unusual to see a variety of other clothing styles scattered here. The peoples of Qatar are often from foreign lands, and their choice of clothing reflects this diversity.

Qatari men and women have very distinctive styles of dressing.

While some clothing is purchased in department stores, a great deal of it still comes directly from individual dressmakers. Women will go to a favorite seamstress and pick out the fabric and style desired. One day later, a new dress will be ready.

RELIGION

IF THERE IS ONE thing that rules a Qatari's life, it is the belief in Islam. With 93 percent of the people living in this country practicing the Islamic faith, it is clear that this religious philosophy guides everything from what people eat and wear each day to how they do business and obey the law. Although Christians, Hindus, and Buddhists combined make up about 5 percent of the people in Qatar, their belief systems are often overwhelmed by the strong presence of Islam.

ISLAM

Islam is based on the Arabic word *aslama* (Uh-SLAH-mah) that means submission, or surrender, to God's will. For a Muslim, absolutely

Left: **A mosque in Qatar.**

Opposite: **Muslims gathering outside the Ali Bin Ali mosque in Doha for prayers.**

everything in life revolves around faith. In Qatar, Muslims are primarily from the Sunni branch of Islam while the Iranians in the country are Shi'ite Muslims. Despite these differences, they tend to allow each other the space and freedom to believe the way they choose. An Islamic proverb that encourages this states, "Unto you your religion and unto me my religion."

Islam is based on the experience of a man known as the Prophet Muhammad. He founded the religion in the A.D. 600s. He was born in Mecca in A.D. 570. Both of his parents died when he was still a young child. As a youth, he worked as a camel driver and trader, and he was also a husband and father. Suddenly, at the age of 40, Muhammad announced that

Muslims prostrate before Allah as part of the Salat ritual five times a day.

THE FIVE PILLARS OF ISLAM

The life of a Muslim is a disciplined one. Five times a day (dawn, noon, mid-afternoon, sunset, and nightfall) a muezzin (myu-EH-zin), the official who announces the call to prayer, cries out to Muslims to come and pray. The reminder is often broadcast over loudspeakers in some of the most-populated areas.

Before going into a traditional Muslim mosque, men must wash their hands, feet, arms, and face. (Women traditionally pray at home, not in public.) Each man kneels on the ground and faces in the direction of Mecca, the holy city located in Saudi Arabia. People bend over until their heads touch the floor as they pray.

Muslims are expected to carry out five basic duties during their lives. These are known as the Pillars of Islam. They are:

- *shahadah* (sha-ha-DAH): The official declaration, or profession, of faith. This is often said in a prayer that states, "There is no god but God, and Muhammad is the messenger of God."
- *salat* (sah-LAHT): The practice of praying at five designated times each day.
- *zakat* (zah-KAHT): Giving a percentage of one's income and assets to those in need (commonly 2.5 percent of a person's annual income given to places such as orphanages, widows, and other countries in need).
- *saum* (sah-OOM): During the month of Ramadan, the practice of fasting between sunrise and sundown to learn self-discipline, focus on God, and sympathy for the poor. (Children under 12, the elderly, visitors, and pregnant or nursing women are exempt.)
- hajj: If possible, making a pilgrimage to Mecca at least once a year or at least once in a lifetime.

the angel Gabriel visited him, and for the next 22 years followers of Islam believe he learned Allah's most important lessons. All of these messages are in the sacred text, the Koran, or Holy Book of Islam. The principles of Islam state that God is Allah, and that a person would go to heaven or hell based on his or her final judgment. Islam believes in guardian angels and that many different prophets have been sent throughout history to spread the word of Islam. Muhammad was one of these prophets, along with other men, such as Moses, Abraham, and Jesus.

At the time that Muhammad began to preach about this new religion, the people of Mecca were not necessarily pleased, especially when he attempted to rid the city of the shrines set up for other gods. His ideas of charity and equality were not welcomed, and soon he and many of his followers moved away to the city of Yathrib in a migration that came to be known as *hijra* (HID-rah). This occurred in A.D. 622, which became the first year of the Islamic calendar. Years later, when Muhammad and his followers returned to Mecca, they were welcomed.

Islam spread quickly throughout the entire Middle East. In less than 200 years it had gone from Spain to India, making its way

The Koran is considered to be the record of Allah's words to his people.

RELIGIOUS HOLIDAYS

The biggest festival in Qatar is, not surprisingly, linked to Islam. It is known as Eid al-Fitr and it is celebrated when Ramadan, the month of fasting, is over. Ramadan begins with the new moon the ninth month of the Islamic calendar. Some Muslims climb to the top of their houses to see the first possible sight of the new moon. As soon as it is spotted, the holiday begins. They pray and then retire for the night. In the morning, before sunrise, they have a breakfast called *suhur*. It is usually made of bread with mutton. The fast continues until dusk, when it is broken by a sip of water. After prayers, a full dinner called iftar (IF-tahr) is eaten.

When Ramadan finally comes to an end, Muslims celebrate with Eid al-Fitr, which means "festival of breaking the fast." During this time, houses are decorated, gifts are bought, money is given to the poor, and people put on new clothes. When they see each other, they embrace three times. A prayer called the *Salat al-id* (sahlaht-al-EED) is recited in the mosques. Parties are held. Although alcohol and dancing are forbidden, people still have a wonderful time. Feasts are eaten and special sweet treats are served (*below*), including a sugary mint drink called *sekanjabin* (She-KAHN-jah-bean). Eid al-Fitr is also a time of forgiving all past grudges and arguments. It is much like an all-new beginning.

from country to country with traders on ships, missionaries, and soldiers. Believers were called Muslims. Some of Islam's most important sayings and traditions were noted down and called *Hadith* (heh-DEETH).

Examples of these types of sayings include:

"One learned man is more difficult for Satan than a thousand worshippers."

"He who wisheth to enter the Paradise at the best door must please his father and mother."

"Actions of a person will be judged according to the person's intentions."

"Assist any person oppressed, whether Muslim or non-Muslim."

"Richness does not lie in the abundance of worldly goods but richness is the richness of the soul (heart, self)."

The *Hadith* is a collection of significant sayings and traditions of Islam.

THE LIFE CYCLE OF A MUSLIM

When a Muslim child is born into a family, some set traditions are usually observed. At birth, the summons to prayer is whispered in the child's right ear so that it is the first sound the child hears. At the same time, the *shahada* or profession of faith is whispered in the left ear. Often a reading from the Koran is included. The new baby is not named until the sixth or seventh day at an official naming ceremony. Family and friends gather together, and a lock of hair is cut from the infant's head. This naming ritual is also considered an entrance rite to the Islamic faith.

Muslims believe that death is a departure from life on this world, but not the end of existence itself, which continues with eternal life with God.

When a Muslim is getting close to death, others gather round him to give comfort and prayer. They will also encourage him to say "I bear witness that there is no god but Allah" right before death, if possible. Once the person dies, the others continue to pray and make preparations for the funeral. Everyone remains calm because

Muslim children are taught from birth that Islam is a way of life and not just a religion.

screaming or crying excessively is forbidden. Normal displays of grief are permitted based on the Prophet Mohammad's response when his son died. "Verily my eyes shed tears and my heart is afflicted, and I say nothing except what is pleasing to my Benefactor." It is not the Muslim's place to question God about death.

Typically, Muslims are buried within the day of the death. In preparation the family or other members of the community wash the body with scented water and then shroud it in sheets of clean, white cloth known as *kafan* (kah-FAHN).

Next the deceased is taken to the site for funeral prayers called *salaatul janaazah* (sah-lah-ah-TOOL jah-nah-ah-ZAH). Everyone prays for the person, and then the men take the body to the gravesite. The body is placed facing toward Mecca, and markers are rarely placed

THE WORLD OF HINDUS

Although Hindus are certainly the minority in this Muslim country, they do live in Qatar and continue to worship in their own way. Hindus believe in one Supreme Being, as well as the concept of *karma,* (KAR-mah) or the law of cause and effect that every person creates with his thoughts, words, and deeds. In addition, Hindus believe that people's souls are reincarnated repeatedly until they reach *moksha* (MAHK-shah), and their liberation is reached. Because Hindus believe that all life is sacred and meant to be loved and respected, they practice *ahimsa* (uh-HIM-sah), the philosophy of not hurting anyone or anything through thoughts, actions, or words. They tend to be very tolerant of other religions, believing that no one religion is the way to find God, but that each one is a path that deserves tolerance and understanding.

FINDING CHRISTIANITY IN QATAR

In 2004 for the first time since the 7th century, a Christian church was built in Doha. The land for the Catholic church, The Parish of Saint Mary of the Rosary, was donated by the emir. At the same time, he also gave land to the Protestants, Anglicans, and other Christian denominations to build their own churches. Archbishop Giuseppe de Andrea from Kuwait was there to see the construction on the new parish begin. He said, "This is a historic moment, an event of grace for the Church in this part of the world."

there. The family mourns for three days, which includes having visitors over and wearing simple clothing. If a woman has just lost her husband, her mourning period, acording to the Koran, should last 3 months and 10 days. During this time, she has to remain single, stay in her home, and wear plain clothes and jewelry.

Women at a grave saying prayers for the deceased.

شارع علي بن عبد الله

Ali Bin Abdulla

7

07

ST
138

LANGUAGE

ONE OF THE FIRST challenges outsiders face when coming to Qatar is simply how to pronounce the name of the country. It seems like it should sound like "guitar," but that is not correct. It sounds closer to "cutter" or "gutter," but in the end, most foreigners simply will not pronounce it properly because of the way the Arabic language is spoken.

THE OFFICIAL LANGUAGE

By far, the primary language heard throughout Qatar is Arabic. Although the country is made up more of foreigners than locals, most of them came from Arabic-speaking countries as well. The other languages spoken include English, Farsi, and Urdu.

Left: **The primary language in Qatar is Arabic, which is also one of the most difficult languages to learn.**

Opposite: **Road signs in Qatar are written both in Arabic and its romanized form.**

Arabic is considered to be the second-hardest language in the world to learn. It is second only to Chinese. Its pronunciation and the way the letters are put together are extremely alien to anyone who speaks a European-based language, including Americans. Even the look of Arabic is unfamiliar. It has a cursive alphabet with letters that look more like pieces of art than words. The letters are always joined together unless used in signs where the words are written vertically. To make things even more complicated, Arabic is written and read from right to left.

The Arabic language dates all the way back to the 4th century when it was first used. It is not only the language of a region; it is the language of a religion. It is the language used in recording Muhammad's

SOME FAMILIAR WORDS

Most people may think they do not know any Arabic, but over the centuries, some words from that language have evolved and made their way into common English terms. Look at this list. How many words seem familiar?

algebra	gazelle	safari
algorithm	ghoul	sesame
almanac	giraffe	sherbet
apricot	guitar	spinach
caliber	henna	sultan
carafe	jasmine	tambourine
carob	lilac	typhoon
checkmate	magazine	zenith
cipher	massage	zero
coffee	monsoon	

teachings in Islam's main book, the Koran. The Koran is written in literary or very close to classical Arabic, the form of Arabic used in media, such as news, television, books, magazines, and newspapers. The other type of Arabic is "colloquial" or dialectal Arabic, which is what is used in daily discussions and casual conversations. It is also the language that might be heard on informal television shows, such as soap operas and talk shows. Colloquial Arabic varies greatly from one place to another, sometimes these dialect groups are different to the point of being incomprehensible to other Arab speakers.

The Arabic alphabet has 28 letters and while words are written in lines from right to left, numbers are written from left to right. The form of the letters change based on their position in the beginning, middle, and end of a word, or simply when standing alone.

COMMON WORDS AND PHRASES

Here are some frequently used words and phrases in Arabic.

Good morning	*Sabah al-kheir*
Good evening	*Masa al-kheir*
Hello	*Marhaba*
Bye	*Ma-as-salamah*
Yes	*Na'am*
No	*La*
Please	*Min fadlak* to a man, *Min fadlik* to a woman
What is your name?	*Shismak?*
Thank you	*Shukran*

QATARI POETRY AND LITERATURE

Although poetry is an important tradition in Qatar, there is very little of it actually written down. Instead, thanks to their Bedouin heritage, many people depend on oral tradition to pass poems from person to person. The National Library in Doha is supervised by the National Council of Culture, Arts, and Heritage that has a number of responsibilities, some of which include storing Qatari heritage, organizing local book fairs, and providing book lending services to the public. In addition to this, it also procures various publications as well as exchanges information and other data with various centers and libraries in other locations. The library is located next to the National Council for Culture, Arts, and Heritage in Doha. It contains a history and Science museum.

One of Qatar's most well-known writers is Captain Abdul Rahim Al Siddiqi. An airline pilot by profession, he is also an author of poems, stories, and scripts. In an interview with *Explore Qatar,* he speaks of his passion for the written word and how he ended up as a pilot. When he set his sights on going to the United States to study film, he could not find a way to do it. A friend suggested that he become a pilot so that he could travel where he wanted. "Flying opened my mind to new cultures and made me adapt to new surroundings and people," he explained. His original inspiration to write came from his parents. "My father always had a huge library, and ever since I was in school I loved to read and write," he said. "My father encouraged me to give in my poems to the local newspaper and after that I have never looked back."

So far, Al Siddiqi has written six books about Arab society, as well as ten plays for children. He has written scripts for television and for the Qatar theatre. One of those plays has been translated into English. Al Siddiqi would like to encourage more of the Qatari people to read: He said,

I hope we can revive reading habits in kids and young adults. Its [*sic*] not easy, but if at home parents ask children to read instead of letting them watch TV, I am sure it can make a difference . . . . I think its [*sic*] up to the parents and teachers to bring out the child's potential and creativity. Constant encouragement, a conducive environment, and the passion for art will help new writers and poets to develop. So, it's up to each nation and cultural community to figure out a way to promote their culture-writers, poets, and artists being an integral part of it.

TELEVISION AND THE PENINSULA

In late 1996 a new television station called Al-Jazeera, or The Peninsula, began broadcasting from the Middle East. Qatar gave them a grant to get started. The Peninsula was established following a controversial

---

QATAR'S DAILY NEWSPAPER

In 1978 Gulf Publishing & Printing Company founded *The Gulf Times* daily newspaper. The first edition was published on December 10, 1978. At first it was a weekly paper. By early 1981, however, it was printed daily. Today it is considered to be the premier English-language publication in Qatar.

In a speech by the late Sheikh Ali ibn Jabor al-Thani, the founding chairman of the board, he said,

It is fair to say that our Company is a cornerstone of the Qatari information media. Since its inception it has been dedicated to reflecting events at home and abroad. Always, our watchwords have been truth and accuracy. We have opened our columns to debate; offered distinguished journalism and useful information. We conceive our publications as offering a stream of knowledge: artistic, literary, political and financial. They are, we hope, a focal point of thought and culture. We maintain a continuous creative effort to serve the country and its citizens, striving to reach new horizons but approaching that task with responsibility, fairness, balance and honesty.

argument between the British Broadcasting Corporation (BBC) and Saudi Arabia's Orbit Communications. When the BBC insisted on the right to show the news as it happened, without censorship, Orbit pulled its sponsorship. The emir, who had already gotten rid of the Ministry of Information, the source of censorship in Saudi Arabia and most Arab nations, said that Al-Jazeera should "report the news as they see it." He added, "I believe criticism can be a good thing and some discomfort for government officials is a small price to pay for this new freedom."

Men at work in the broadcast room of Al-Jazeera television station.

Al-Jazeera
Exclusive

خـاص
بالجزيرة

أولى
حروب القرن

أسـامـة بـن لادن
زعيم تنظيم القاعدة

A frame from the video message that Al-Jazeera broadcasted from terrorist leader Osama Bin Laden.

Because the television station is completely free of any censorship or government control, it has become known throughout the world as a reputable and respected source of information. It shocked people from the first day it went on the air by bringing up topics and issues for debate that were rarely even spoken of in public. It opened new avenues for debate and freedom of thought.

However, Al-Jazeera has not been without its critics. Some United Kingdom media sources call it the "mouthpiece" of known terrorist leader Osama Bin Laden and the terror group, al-Qaeda. It was at this station that the infamous al-Qaeda leader dropped his anonymous videotape on his message of terror. U.S. officials have shown concern in the past that the station has a definite anti-Western tone in many of its reports. During the Afghan war, the Al-Jazeera bureau in Kabul was bombed by the United States, as was the bureau in Baghdad during the invasion of Iraq. Later reports stated that President Bush planned to bomb the bureau in Qatar as well, but was dissuaded by Prime Minister Tony Blair of Britain.

In 2006 the station launched an English version, Al Jazeera International, featuring television news professionals from the BBC, CNN, and the Canadian Broadcasting Corp. It has based its programming on the Western model, offering a variety of news programs. One of its most popular shows is "The Opposite Direction," similar to CNN's "Crossfire."

The newsroom of Arabic language news broadcast station Al-Jazeera.

ARTS

THE QATARI MAKE SOME OF the most beautiful handicrafts in the world. They are known for many different types, thanks to the influence of different cultures and their nomadic background. The capital city features some of the most fascinating museums and theaters in the world. They are enjoyed by citizens as well as tourists alike.

Some of the Qatari homemade handicraft that have passed from one generation to another include woven rugs, embroidered cloth, and baskets made out of palm leaves. Women are also quite skilled at dying goat and camel hair, and weaving them into unique and decorative camel bags and bedding. Special cloth is made with gold thread to create unusual patterns and fancy designs. All of these handiworks tend to be beautiful but also practical, a throwback to the ancient Bedouin culture when anything that was made had to be useful or it was left behind.

Above: **Bedouin jewelry is traditionally made out of silver and adorned with precious stones.**

Opposite: **Patterns on Bedouin tapestry is a good example of how the Qataris turn nature into a fine piece of art.**

MUSIC AND DANCE

Along with handicraft, the Qatari also appreciate music and dance of a particular genre. Traditional songs performed by folksingers and musicians are common at weddings and other national celebrations. Qatari music and dance reflects their lifestyle, as they live with the salty sea and windy deserts. Before the discovery of oil transformed their nation, music was often the main method of entertainment. It passed stories from one generation to the next and unified the people's struggle in a harsh and demanding land.

After that struggle ended, the music began to change as well. Lyrics reflected people's comfort and contentment, dance movements still sometimes mimicked the physical efforts of the past, such as fishing or pearling.

One of the most popular dances performed throughout the Arab Emirates is the *liwa* (LEE-wah), which originated from the coast of East Africa. It features a pipe-like flute called a *mizmar* (mihz-MAHR).

THE THEATER OF QATAR

Qatar's theater history is intense but also quite new. It was not until 1972 that the Qatar Theater Troup was formed. The following year it was followed by another group known as the al-Sadd Theatrical Troupe. Two other troupes followed and in 1994, all four of them merged into two major groups known as the Qatar Theatrical Troupe and the Doha Theatrical Troupe. Through the government's Culture and Arts Department, theater scholars from other countries come to Qatar to share their expertise, and Qatari theater trainees travel to other Arab countries to learn from troupes there. Each year on March 27 Qatar celebrates International Theater Day. Entertainment is offered all day to show what the actors and actresses have learned about the performing arts in the previous year.

It sounds like an oboe and comes in two pieces. Drums are also used in this dance. With the *liwa*, both men and women are allowed to dance. Although it starts out slow, the pace of the music increases until it is quite fast by the time it ends almost a half hour later.

While some of the dances have set steps, there are others that are more free in form and creative. People jump up in the air or move

Men performing the Raza warrior dance, which is an example of a dance with fixed dance steps.

in all directions. Women even have their own dances, including the *al-khimar* (ahl KEE-mahr), in which either a single woman or several women dance with colorful veils across their faces. A single male sometimes performs the *ar-razif* (ahr-rah-ZEFF), in which he wields a sword, a rifle, or a dagger and stomps on the ground with his feet.

The instruments used for most performances are drums. The Indian drum is a wooden one covered in leather and wrapped with ropes. Another drum that first came from Africa is one that stands

The Indian drum is an instrument that is frequently used as accompaniment for many Qatari performances.

THE AYYALAH SONG AND DANCE

Perhaps one of the most impressive performances in all of Qatar is the *ayyalah* (eye-YAH-lah). It is often done at weddings, on National Day, and to celebrate the end of Ramadan. More than just a dance, it tells of their history, represents unity and strength, and the lyrics bring in the concepts of chivalry and courage. It is commonly done to display allegiance to the emir as well. The only instruments used are drums, cymbals and tambourines. The large, lead drum is known as the *al-ras* (ahl-RAHS). Smaller *takhamir* (tahk-ha-MEER) drums provide a soft sound. Some of the drums are played with sticks, while other performers just use their hands or a combination of both.

The number of men performing the dance varies greatly. At least 60 dancers participate, but there are usually more. They stand in two rows and face each other, with arms linked and holding swords. They sway back and forth to the beat of the drums and each row alternates singing a challenge or boast to the other side. Often a poet will walk between the two lines of men, reciting lines that they then echo.

on three legs and is covered on top with goat skin. The *al-mirwa* is a small drum that is held with one hand and beaten with the fingers. Along with drums, the Qataris also use the *al-sirnai,* a large wind instrument made out of a hollowed out reed with holes and a *rebec,* a stringed instrument played with a bow that is commonly made from horsetail hair. The *tambura* (tahm-BOO-rah) is a cousin to early harps. It has five strings made out of horse gut and they are stretched out between a wooden base covered in camel skin. The strings are actually plucked with a sheep's horn that has been especially treated and shaped just for this purpose. The tambura makes a sound similar to a bass violin.

The *manior* is another instrument used in Qatari music. It is a percussion instrument similar to a drum, but in this case, in order for people to play it, they have to wear it. It is made out of thick cotton and covered with hundreds of loosely stitched, dried goat's hooves. By putting this instrument on like a skirt and then jumping, twisting, and turning, the musician can create a unique clapping sound. The *alhaban* (ahl-ha-BAHN) is similar to a bagpipe attached to a piece of goatskin. It is so awkward to play that the musician's struggle is often as much a part of the performance as the sound the pipes make.

DEPARTMENT OF MUSEUMS AND ARCHAEOLOGY

There are a number of museums throughout Qatar, including the Qatar National Museum, the Maritime Museum, the Weaponry Museum, the Doha Fort, and several others.

Opposite: **A man playing the *tambura*.**

Below: **The National Museum of Qatar.**

One of the most impressive museums will be the Museum of Islamic Art. When it is completed, it will be one of the most notable landmarks in Islamic heritage in the world. Designed by Chinese-American architect I.M. Pei, it should be completed by the summer of 2007.

Exhibits on display in a museum in Qatar.

A MUSEUM OF WEAPONS

In the Al Laqta area is a museum that contains displays of more than 2,000 rare and historical gilded swords, curved daggers (*below*), shiny armor, and powerful rifles dating back to the 16th century. The Islamic weapons are divided into two categories. The first includes individual weapons, such as arrows and other defensive weapons. The second is made up of big and heavy weapons such as machine guns. Along with the weapons, the museum also has a number of presents on display that were given to the country by presidents and other heads of state or bought at international auctions.

The museum will cover an amazing 340,000 square feet (31,587 sq m) and will be located on the southern portion of the Corniche in Doha. It will be visible from all directions and will even have its own marina for guests who come by boat.

Inside, the new museum will feature a number of permanent and temporary exhibition halls, a specialized library, a reading hall, and an educational center. The Islamic Museum will display the Qatar National Collection of Islamic Art, a collection of ceramics, metal work, jewelry, wood work, glass, and other Islamic crafts made from Spain to Central Asia. Artifacts of ivory and silk will be displayed, some of which date back more than 600 years. The museum's management only hope that this museum will help people to recognize and appreciate the impact of Islam on the rest of the world.

ARABIC OPERA

In 2003 Qatari theater fans were treated to a first: an opera written and produced by Arabs. With an audience of 3,000, the performance was held in open air and told the story of love and treason in the 10th century. Performed in English the first night, the following weeks of shows were done in Arabic.

Avicenna, written by Qatari scholar Dr. Ahmad al-Doari, centers on the life of a philosopher and doctor who lived during the Middle Ages. The costumes and elaborate sets were made out of colorful silk, satin, and taffeta. At the end of the performance, al-Dosari came out on the stage and said, "Opera has no nationality, no country. It is universal: this is our message."

A NEW DIRECTION FOR QATARI FASHION

In the spring of 2006 graduates of the Virginia Commonwealth University School of the Arts in Qatar and Qatari fashion designers Noor Hamad al-Thani and Noor Jassim al-Thani put on a fashion show under their new label of "Noors." With the motto: "Design is a flower awaiting your attention to blossom," their styles were a big hit with the crowd. They presented everything from designs for the working woman to elegant eveningwear. Both of the women have won multiple awards in different countries for their fashion designs. Sponsored by Salam International Company Limited, the show was meant to be a way for Qatari women to blend work and style. A spokesperson from the company said, "The show is another first for Salem International and Noor and Noor, who are starting together on a road less traveled."

Qatari fashion is Arabian with a modern yet exotic beauty to it.

LEISURE

BECAUSE QATAR IS SUCH a prosperous country, most of the people living there have quite a bit of free time and money to spend on fun and relaxation. In the mid-1990s the government's Youth Authority showed its strong support of sports by sponsoring a number of clubs and associations that promote a variety of sports, including bowling, table tennis, martial arts, basketball, cricket, billiards, and even chess. Thanks to good weather and a lot of sun, there are a lot of sporting options to choose from. Runners and bikers enjoy the Corniche. Boaters and fishers have endless waters to spend time on. The options do not end there, however.

Locals and tourists alike enjoy watching the sport of camel racing. While normally used in the past for transport, today camels are used more around the track than anywhere else. Although they may look awkward, camels can reach speeds of up to 25 miles per hour (40 km per hour) as they race around the three- to six-mile (five- to ten-km) track. No betting is allowed, but there are hundreds of thousands of dollars in prizes, thanks to corporate sponsors.

Just recently the sport was made even more interesting when the government invested more than $1 million in creating an all-new kind of jockey. In the past, many countries, including Qatar, had a terrible

Above: **Young boys participate as jockeys for camel races.**

Opposite: **Soccer is one of Qatar's favorite sports.**

Jockeys training at the Nad Al Sheba racetrack in prepartion for the Dubai Kahayla Classic race.

reputation for stealing small children and forcing them to live and work as jockeys. This practice was condemned by multiple human rights groups; since 2005 the young jockeys have been replaced with something entirely different—robots. Instead of humans, these jockeys are made out of titanium and look like small people. They are operated by remote control. They are able to shout at the camels and even use whips. By 2007 they will be the only jockeys on the track.

Of course, the more traditional horse racing is also popular in Qatar. The royal family is a big supporter of the sport. The sandy desert is host to both local and international 26-mile (42-km) desert marathons that capture everyone's attention as riders take to the sand in endurance races.

SOCCER AND WATER SPORTS

Like many other countries, Qataris are huge fans of soccer. There are 16 soccer clubs in the country and each one has its own stadium. In 1996 the national soccer team even reached the quarter finals at the summer Olympics in Barcelona, Spain. Soccer player Jay-Jay Okocha plays for the national team today.

All of the water in Qatar attract boaters. Dhows, or wooden sailing boats (many of which are made right on the shoreline) are a common sight. The waters off Qatar's shores attract a number of international boat races, and regular regattas are held during most months of the

Players from Qatar's Al-Saad club celebrate their win of the Crown Prince Cup in Doha.

WHEN NATURE AND MAN MEET

Few sports in Qatar are as respected and cherished as the custom of falconry. It is an art, a tradition, and a hobby all rolled into one. It dates back more than 3,000 years. While some areas of the world have given up this sport, the people of Qatar have held on to it determinedly. Fathers train their sons and in the process, try to impart the values of courage, patience, and dedication along with it.

Falcons have been a symbol of bravery and beauty to the Arab world for hundreds of years. They were a vital part of Bedouin life in the past. These birds often brought much-needed food to a sparse and rather monotonous diet by helping in the hunt for other animals.

Catching a falcon is no easy job. They come to the Arabian area when they migrate, and then are carefully trapped. For the next few weeks the handlers, or falconers, as the people who train and use falcons are called, work hard to create a strong bond of trust between themselves and the wild birds. This requires daily human contact. Occasionally falcons will wear hoods until they have gotten used to being handled by humans.

The handlers commonly buy whatever equipment they need at some of the local souqs to take care of their birds. This may include a bell or pair of bells for the birds to wear on their legs, strong leather straps, and protective gloves.

Training is a slow process known as *meqnas,* or hunting journey. The falconer must have a strong knowledge of the desert, its heat, and terrain, as well as a strong understanding of the bird he is training. Hunting season begins in autumn and continues throughout the winter until early spring. The falcons commonly chase down a bird called "houbara bustard," which migrates through the area each autumn. It is a large, fast-flying bird about the size of a heron. Many Qataris think its meat is delicious.

The hunt begins with the falcon delicately perched on its handler's arm. At the given signal, the bird takes flight to chase its prey. The falconer must keep track of the falcon. These birds can reach speeds of up to 62 miles per hour (100 km per hour) and when they dive, they can easily double that. The handler must be located within a few seconds of the falcon's landing so that there is no fighting between the bird and its prey. This prevents the bird from being injured in any way. In the past, falconers kept up with their birds by camel or horseback. Today it is typically done in a jeep.

year. Another popular event is the annual race of long boats. Natually, swimmers also enjoy the water. Water skiing, wind surfing, scuba diving, and snorkeling are all popular sports.

WELCOME TO THE GAMES

In December 2006 Qatar hosted the 15th Annual Asian Games. This was quite an honor. Qatar had to compete with a number of other Asian cities for the position and it succeeded in getting the most votes. This made Doha the first city in its region and only the second in West Asia to host this prestigious event. The Asian Games are the

Yachts off the waters of Qatar competing in The Oryx Quest—a nonstop race around the world beginning and ending in the Middle East.

second-largest international sporting event in the world, following the Olympic Games.

The country invested in preparation for the games. They expanded the airport and added hotels. They built Khalifa Sports City, which features a stadium that can hold 50,000 spectators, an aquatic center, and a huge indoor sports hall with a dome.

In addition, an Athlete's Village was built to house the thousands of athletes attending the games. It is in the center of Doha, near shopping centers, hospitals, and other helpful services. Once the

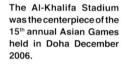

The Al-Khalifa Stadium was the centerpiece of the 15th annual Asian Games held in Doha December 2006.

PART OF THE OLYMPICS

Qatar has participated in the Olympics since the event was held in Montreal in 1976. In that year only a delegation of officials attended. Soon, they began to officially enter athletes. Below is a list of events that Qatar has participated in over the years:

1984	Los Angeles	soccer, athletics, shooting
1988	Seoul	athletics
1992	Barcelona	athletics*, football
1996	Atlanta	athletics, shooting, volleyball
2000	Sydney	athletics, weightlifting*, volleyball, swimming, shooting
2004	Athens	athletics, shooting, weightlifting, swimming

*Won a bronze medal

The mascot for the 2006 Asian Games held in Doha.

games ended, the village was turned into a state of the art medical facility.

The Asian Games lasted for 15 days, and 39 different sports were represented, including water polo, fencing, and sailing. Over 10,000 athletes came to Qatar representing 45 countries and regions. The mascot, Orry the Oryx, carried the torch to start the games. "Sport ties a nation together," said Abdulla Khalid al-Qahtani, director general of the Doha Asian Games Organizing Committee. "It transcends culture while celebrating our diversity. This was a once in a lifetime opportunity for Qatar to demonstrate to the rest of the world just what we can do. In less than 100 days."

Women have an important role in Qatari sports as well. In 2001 the Qatar Women Sports Committee (QWSC) was founded by Sheikh Tamim ibn Hamad al-Thani, president of the Qatar National Olympic Committee. This gave many young women the opportunity to follow their sporting interests. Thanks to the hard work of Dr. Anisa al-Hitmi, who is also president of the QWSC, there are now four women's sports centers in Qatar. Since the organization's start, Qatari women have won medals in table tennis and chess.

For many avid golfers, Doha is a great place for their favorite sport. The Qatar Masters PGA European Tour Event is an annual world-class golf tournament that attracts some of the biggest names in the sport. The course has hosted the Masters since 1998. It was the first-ever grass course in this dry country. It covers 369 acres

Retief Goosen (*right*) of South Africa and Australian Richard Green congratulate one another at the Qatar Golf Masters Tournament.

and it has 1,300 palm trees, 65 cacti, 5,000 shrubs, and 10,000 trees. For a country with little rain, the course requires a lot of extra care to maintain. Qatar is also host to a number of other international sporting events, including a motorcycle grand prix called the Qatar MotoGP. These races began in 2004. The track is 3.3 miles (5.4 km) long with a straightaway that is .66 of a mile (1.068 km) long, allowing racers to speed to 250 miles (402 km per hour.)

READY TO GO SKIING?

In a land where the temperatures rarely dip below 60°F, even in the middle of winter, and the terrain is quite flat, it may be hard to imagine strapping on some skis, grabbing a couple of poles, and rushing downhill. However, that is exactly what a number of sports enthusiasts do in Qatar.

FESTIVALS

THE PEOPLE IN QATAR celebrate primarily Islamic holidays. In September they also celebrate National Day or Independence Day. As the government continues to encourage tourists to come to Qatar, their festivals have taken on more importance. They are becoming less focused on personal festivities and more determined in attracting people from other places to see the wonders and beauty of their peninsula.

SUMMER WONDERS

One of the most anticipated celebrations each year is the fairly new Summer Wonders Festival. Held each summer in Doha, this monthlong festivity attracts millions of tourists. It was created by the Qatar Tourism Authority. It is held in a variety of places throughout the city, including malls and hotels. The official mascot for the event is Bshara, a large, stuffed oryx that entertains children with a combination of laser light shows and fireworks. Entertainment from all over the world is offered at the Qatar International Exhibition Center. Stalls display handicrafts from more than 20 different countries, and music comes from all directions.

In Fun City, families enjoy themselves at puppet shows, rides, and performances by jugglers. The Exhibition Center houses the popular Snow City, where the temperature is below zero. People who live in heat year-round get the chance to make snowballs, build a snowman, or go ice skating. A Russian Circus performs daily as well. Acrobats and clowns amaze and amuse onlookers.

In the Qatari Village, visitors can get a realistic glimpse of how life used to be like in the country. They can see craftspeople of all kinds weaving baskets, making lace, or engraving metals. The Sea Corner is

Opposite: **Qatari men taking part in one of Qatar's numerous festivals.**

also open for people to walk through and learn about the seafaring ways of the Qatari. A Wax Museum lets tourists have face-to-face meetings with wax celebrities such as Madonna and Marilyn Monroe.

During the Summer Wonders Festival, stores and malls offer discounts and prize giveaways. Each year it is a huge success for everyone involved. CEO Fred van Eijk said, "With direction from the leadership of Qatar, QTA (Qatar Tourism Authority) is committed to enhancing tourism and investments and to substantially enhance Qatar's growing reputation worldwide. Our mission is . . . raising global awareness of Qatar as a first class destination for leisure and business," he added.

A young boy enjoys a feast with family and friends.

CELEBRATING ISLAM

Since the majority of the people of Qatar are Muslim, some of the biggest celebrations focus on this religion. Because they use a lunar calendar rather than the traditional one, the actual date of these celebrations vary by a few days from year to year.

Eid Al-Adha usually occurs at the end of December or beginning of January. It is considered to be a celebration of sacrifice. A lamb

A local enjoying the Islamic festivities with a large meal.

or sheep are traditionally sacrificed on this holiday. One-third goes toward feeding the family, while the other two-thirds go to relatives and friends, as well as to the poor. Many Qatari visit friends and share gifts with children. They greet each other with the traditional "Eid mubarak," which translates into "blessed festival" or a way of saying "May your religious holiday be blessed." The day is spent largely in prayer. Schools and businesses are all closed as well.

Sheep like these are traditionally sacrificed during Eid Al-Adha.

One of the nation's other important Islamic holidays is Eid al-Fitr or Festival of Fast-Breaking, which follows the long period of fasting for Ramadan. Muslims the world over spend this time celebrating with family and friends in the spirit of blessings and renewal as this is also a period during which old wrongs are forgiven. This spirit of renewal from fasting and forgiving, as well as seeking pardon lends this festivity an added air of serenity and happiness.

The day typically begins in prayer, followed by a sermon. Then families scatter in different directions to visit loved ones who live nearby and to call those that are not staying near. Gifts are often given to children, new clothes are worn, and feasts are served and eaten. For several days, school is closed. As with Eid Al-Adha, greetings are exchanged, including "Eid Saeed," or "Happy Eid," and Kul'am wa enta bi-khair!," or "May every year find you in good health!"

HONORING INDEPENDENCE

In late August the buildings and streets of Qatar take on a new look as the government decorates them with lights and banners. It is almost time to celebrate.

The festivities begin on September 1 when the Qatari go to the royal palace to honor the emir. At noon a colorful military show and air force performances thrill visitors and locals alike. That evening, restaurants serve some of their best dishes. For the next two days, almost all of Qatar puts work aside in order to celebrate the anniversary of their independence from Great Britain in 1971. Folk dancers fill up the Corniche with dancing and music, while many artists perform the traditional dance of the Ardha.

FOOD

A CLOSE LOOK AT the food served in Qatar provides a glimpse into its history. Traditional Egyptian meals are found here, and many of the dishes are based on the nomadic cooking style of the Bedouins. With such a large influx of foreign workers, however, new cuisine is being added from those who came from Iran, India, and North Africa.

THREE MEALS A DAY

A typical breakfast, or *al-futuur,* in Qatar is yogurt, or *laban,* cheese, along with olives and fruit. It is a light meal served early in the morning before the day's heat has a chance to begin.

Lunch, or *al-ghada,* is the main meal and is usually served just about 1:00 in the afternoon. It features multiple courses and is often served from a large, communal platter. Much of it is eaten by hand, rather than with utensils. A piece of bread is held in the right hand only, and used to scoop up other foods. Lunch often includes a dish made with rice, lamb, or both, along with appetizers, bread, stew, and vegetables. *Ghuzi* is a main dish made of a whole roasted lamb on a bed of rice with pine nuts. *Shawarma* (shah-WAHR-mah) is grilled slivers of lamb or chicken wrapped in lettuce leaves and put into pockets of bread called pita. Other lamb dishes include *matchbous,* which is spiced lamb with rice, and *hareis,* or slow-cooked wheat and lamb. *Wara enab* is a meal of grape leaves stuffed with ground meat and rice, while *koussa mahshi* is a side dish of stuffed zucchini. Since Qatar is surrounded by ocean, seafood is also quite popular here.

Above: **Unleavened bread is a staple among Qataris.**

Opposite: **Fresh produce at a market in Doha.**

A PASSION FOR TRUFFLES

An underground, irregular-shaped fungus with an odd smell, that is related to the mushroom, does not sound like something a person would actively go searching for, but in Qatar, hunting for truffles is an art. A long-standing tradition in this country, the secret of how to find the best truffles is often handed down from one generation to another.

Truffle hunters usually work in teams and start out early in the morning before the sun gets too hot. Truffles are hard to find, and it takes a good eye and determination to succeed. This fungus, which is considered a gourmet delicacy, is usually only found in spots that are warm and moist. In a country with very little rainfall, that is more than a little challenging. Truffle hunters often wait for the rare rainstorm and then head out to track down the "truffle thunder plant."

Truffles typically grow just a few inches below the soil and have neither roots nor leaves. They are found in bunches of 10 to 20. The most common type of truffle in Qatar is the *jubei* or black truffle.

Once found, these tasty morsels are either taken home for cooking in a special meal or sold in local markets. Qatari women like to wash and cut the truffles before cooking them with rice. They are served with bread and butter. Everyone appreciates truffles because they are so rare since they only return with the rain.

Crab, lobster, tuna, shrimp, and snapper are common. Because of the people's religious belief, pork is not eaten.

Chickpeas are used to make hummus which is a frequent dinner treat.

The entire family gathers for this large lunch. Children come home from school, and men come home from work. Everyone eats and then rests for a while before returning to their duties.

Dinner, or *al-ashe,* is served quite late in the evening and is light. Hummus, a paste made out of chickpeas and sesame seeds, is often served. Sandwiches are common. Like the Bedouins, some of the Qataris's food is simple and easy to pack with them, such as dates and dried meat. Each meal is accompanied by *qahwa,* or thick, rich coffee. It is usually sweetened and spiced with cardamom, and served in tiny, thimble-sized cups. For special occasions, sweet coffee is served. It has saffron, cardamom, and sugar put in it.

Qataris like desserts as well. *El asaraya* is a cheesecake made with cream topping, and *mehalabiya* is a pudding made with pistachio nuts and rosewater. Alcohol is forbidden. Of course, with modern influences and foreign workers continually moving into the area, coffee, snacks, and meals can also be found at places like Starbucks, McDonald's, and Pizza Hut. This shows how global Qatar's food variety has become.

FOOD OF THE EXPATRIATES

Chapati is a staple in the diet of many Pakistanis living in Qatar.

Because so many of the people living in Qatar are from other countries, there is a wide variety of cuisine there. For the Pakistanis, meals often

consist of *chapati* (cheh-PAH-tee), an unleavened bread similar to a Mexican tortilla. Another favorite is *lassy* (LAH-see), a dish that is made from milk in which the curds and butter fat have been removed. Lentils, a type of bean, are often used in soups and side dishes. Pakistanis also like to use many different spices in their dishes, including chili powder, tumeric, paprika, cumin, clovers, saffron, and poppy seeds.

The Indians in Qatar eat some of the same foods, but have their own ways of flavoring them. Curry is a particular favorite and is used in side and main dishes. Indians rely a great deal on vegetables for their meals since many of them are also Hindu who avoid eating beef and pork. While not all Hindus are vegetarians, many follow the Laws of Manu, which state that "no sin is attached to eating flesh, but abstinence bears greater fruits."

Many expatriates from Pakistan like to use saffron to enhance the flavor of their food.

TABBOULEH

This is a traditional main or side dish for the people of Qatar. It is a simple recipe that does not take much time to prepare. While this is the typical way of making the dish, the fruits and nuts can be changed to whatever kind people prefer.

    4 cups bulgur or cracked wheat
    4 cups boiling water
    1 cup mango, diced
    1 bunch green onion, finely diced
    ½ cup almonds, chopped
    Mint leaves and parsley, chopped

Mix the bulgur and boiling water in a large mixing bowl. Allow it to soak at room temperature for 30 minutes. Stir occasionally. Refrigerate until completely cool. Then add mango, green onion, and almonds, and crushed mint leaves and parsley if desired.

UMM ALI

This is a traditional dessert based on Egyptian history. It is similar to the bread pudding found in the United States. It is best served warm with vanilla ice cream on top.

1 (17.25 oz) package frozen puff pastry, thawed
5 cups milk
1 cup white sugar
1 teaspoon vanilla extract
¼–½ cup raisins
¼–½ cup almonds, slivered or finely chopped.
¼ cup pine nuts or hazelnuts, chopped
¼ cup pistachio nuts, chopped
¼– ½ cup sweetened coconut flakes, shredded

Preheat the oven to 400 degrees (204°C). Unroll the puff pastry sheets and place flat on a baking sheet. Bake for 15 minutes in the preheated oven or until the sheets are puffed and golden brown. Break the cooked puff pastry into pieces and place in a large bowl. Add the raisins, almonds, pine nuts, pistachios, and coconut. Toss to mix well. Pour into a 9 x 13 glass baking dish and spread out evenly. Pour the milk into a saucepan and stir in the sugar and vanilla. Heat until hot but not quite boiling. Pour over the mixture in the baking dish. Bake for 15 minutes in the preheated oven. Turn the oven to broil and broil for 2 minutes to brown the top. Remove from the oven and let it stand for 5 minutes. Serve warm with ice cream.

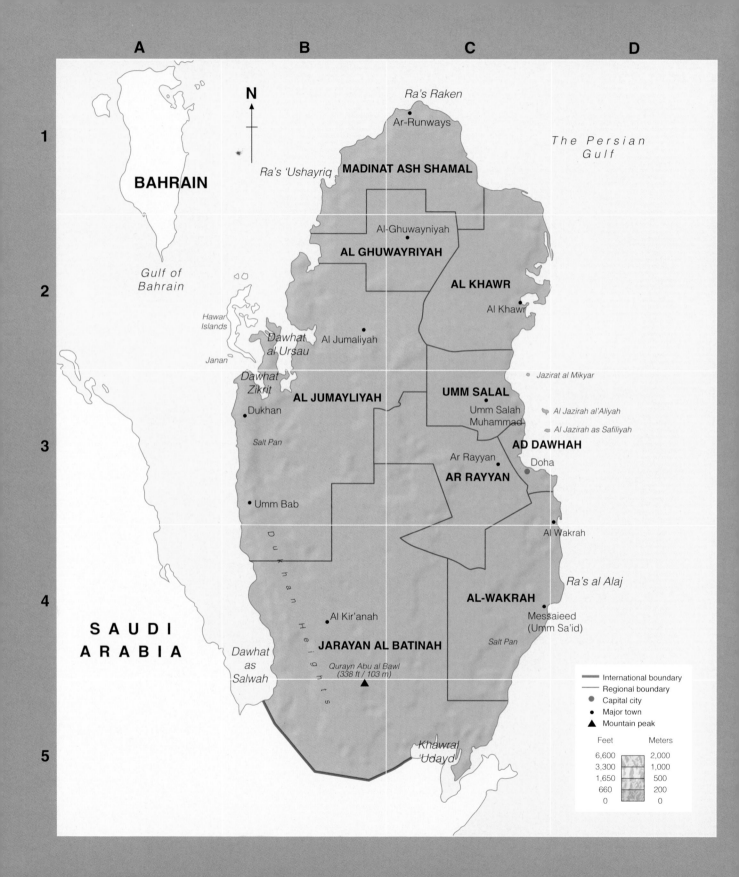

A B C D

1

Ra's Raken

Ar-Runways

The Persian Gulf

Ra's 'Ushayriq

MADINAT ASH SHAMAL

Al-Ghuwayniyah

AL GHUWAYRIYAH

BAHRAIN

AL KHAWR

Al Khawr

2

Gulf of Bahrain

Hawar Islands

Janan

Dawhat al Ursau

Al Jumaliyah

Jazirat al Mikyar

Dawhat Zikrit

AL JUMAYLIYAH

UMM SALAL

Umm Salah Muhammad

Al Jazirah al'Aliyah

Al Jazirah as Safiliyah

Dukhan

AD DAWHAH

Salt Pan

Ar Rayyan

Doha

3

AR RAYYAN

Umm Bab

Al Wakrah

4

Ra's al Alaj

Dukhan Heights

AL-WAKRAH

Al Kir'anah

Messaieed (Umm Sa'id)

JARAYAN AL BATINAH

Salt Pan

Dawhat as Salwah

Qurayn Abu al Bawl (338 ft / 103 m) ▲

S A U D I

A R A B I A

Khawr al Udayd

5

International boundary
Regional boundary
● Capital city
● Major town
▲ Mountain peak

Feet   Meters
6,600   2,000
3,300   1,000
1,650   500
660   200
0   0

MAP OF QATAR

Ad Dawhah, C3, D3

Al Ghuwayriyah City, C2

Al Ghuwayriyah Province, B1, B2, C1, C2

Al Jazirah al'Aliyah, C3

Al Jumayliyah City, B2

Al Jumayliyah Province, B2 - B4, C2, C3

Al Kir'anah, B4

Al Khawr City, C2

Al Khawr Province, C1, C2

Al Wakrah City, D3

Al Wakrah Province, C1–C5, D3, D4

Ar Rayyan City, C3

Ar Rayyan Province, B3, C3, C4

Ar Ruways, C1

Bahrain, A1, A2

Dawhat as Salwah, A3, A4, B4, B5

Dawhat al Ursayn, B2, B3

Dawhat Zikrit, B3

Doha, C3

Dukhan, B3

Dukhan Heights, B4, B5

Gulf of Bahrain, A2

Janan Island, B2

Jarayan Al Batinah, B3–B5, C3–C5

Jazirat al Mikyar, C3

Khor al Udeid, C5

Madinat Ash Shamal, B1, B2, C1, C2

Messaieed Umm Sa'id, C4

Qurayn Abu al Bawl, B5

Ra's al Alaj, D4

Ra's Raken, C1

Ra's Ushayriq, B1

Saudi Arabia, A2–A5, B5, C5

The Persian Gulf, D1– D5

Umm Bab, B3

Umm Salal, C2, C3

Umm Salal Muhammad, C3

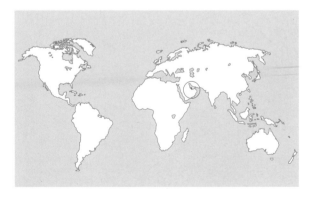

133

ECONOMIC QATAR

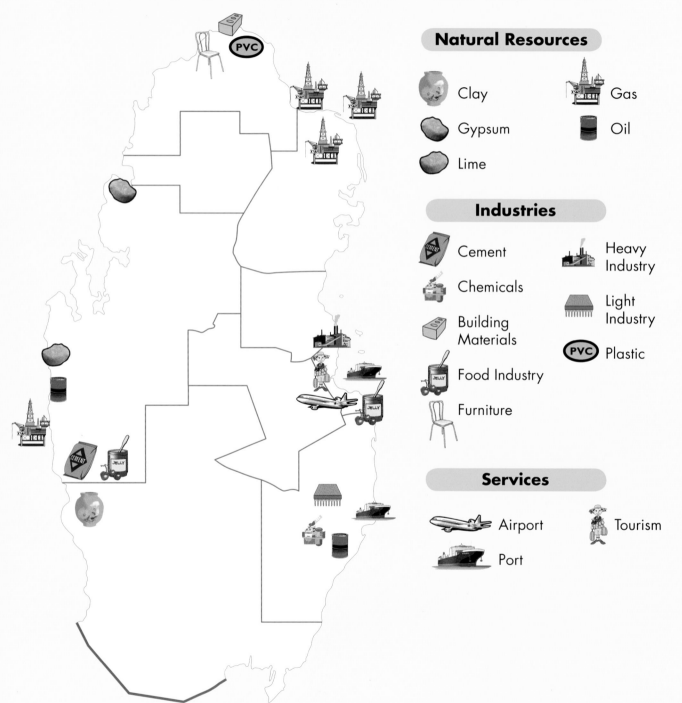

Natural Resources

- Clay
- Gypsum
- Lime
- Gas
- Oil

Industries

- Cement
- Chemicals
- Building Materials
- Food Industry
- Furniture
- Heavy Industry
- Light Industry
- PVC Plastic

Services

- Airport
- Port
- Tourism

ABOUT
THE ECONOMY

OVERVIEW
Qatar has one of the strongest economies in the world. With its exportation of oil and natural gas, this is sure to continue for another 20 years. There is a drive to find new venues for revenue, and foreign investors are both eager and welcomed.

GROSS DOMESTIC PRODUCT (GDP)
$23.64 billion (2005)

GDP SECTORS
Agriculture 0.2 percent, industry 80.1 percent, services 19.7 percent

IMPORTS
$6.706 billion (2005)

EXPORTS
$24.9 billion (2005)

WORKFORCE
440,000 (2005)

UNEMPLOYMENT RATE
2.7% (2001)

CURRENCY
1 Qatari Riyal (QAR) = 100 dirhams
Notes: 1, 5, 10, 50, 100, and 500 riyals
Coins: 1, 5, 10, 25 and 50 dirhams
1 USD = 3.64 QAR (July 2001)

INFLATION RATE
8.8 percent

MAIN INDUSTRIES
Crude oil production and refining, cement, petrochemicals, steel reinforcing bars

AGRICULTURAL PRODUCTS
Fruits, vegetables, poultry, dairy products, beef, fish

MAIN IMPORTS
Transport equipment, food, chemicals

MAIN EXPORTS
Liquified natural gas, petroleum products, fertilizers, steel

TRADE PARTNERS
Japan, South Korea, Singapore, India (2005)

CULTURAL QATAR

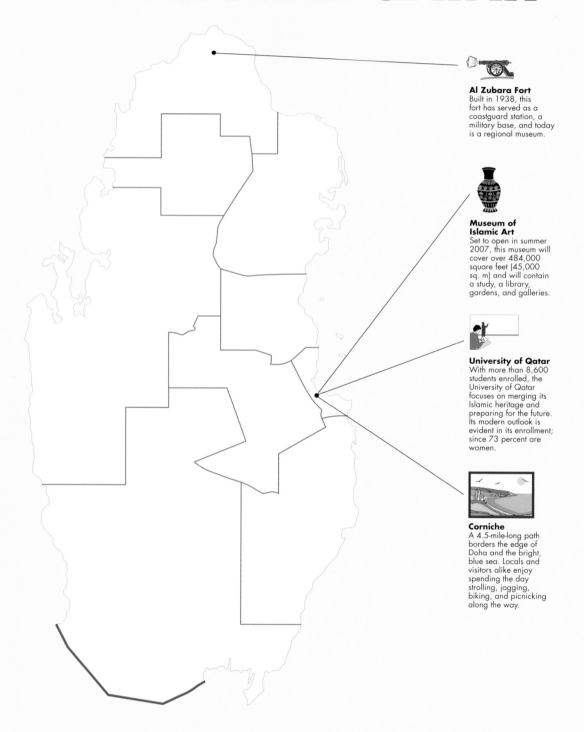

Al Zubara Fort
Built in 1938, this fort has served as a coastguard station, a military base, and today is a regional museum.

Museum of Islamic Art
Set to open in summer 2007, this museum will cover over 484,000 square feet (45,000 sq. m) and will contain a study, a library, gardens, and galleries.

University of Qatar
With more than 8,600 students enrolled, the University of Qatar focuses on merging its Islamic heritage and preparing for the future. Its modern outlook is evident in its enrollment; since 73 percent are women.

Corniche
A 4.5-mile-long path borders the edge of Doha and the bright, blue sea. Locals and visitors alike enjoy spending the day strolling, jogging, biking, and picnicking along the way.

ABOUT
THE CULTURE

COUNTRY NAME
State of Qatar

CAPITAL CITY
Doha

OTHER IMPORTANT CITIES
Ar-Rayyan, Al-Wakrah, Mesaieed

POPULATION
885,359 (July 2006 est.)

ETHNIC GROUPS
Qatari 25 percent; Indian 18 percent; Pakistani 18 percent; Iranian 10 percent; European 29 percent

LIFE EXPECTANCY
73.9 years

LITERACY RATE
89 percent (2006)

MAJOR HOLIDAYS AND FESTIVALS
Eid al-Fitr, following Ramadan; Independence Day

RELIGION
Muslims (95 percent)
Others (5 percent)

RELIGIOUS GROUPS
Muslims (95 percent)
Christians
Hindus
Buddhists
Others (5 percent)

OFFICIAL LANGUAGE
Arabic

TIME LINE

IN QATAR	IN THE WORLD
	753 B.C. Rome is founded
600 B.C. The settlement at Shagra.	
A.D. 200 Rule of Sassanids of Persia.	
	A.D. 600 Height of Mayan civilization
A.D. 628 Qatar accepts the Islam religion.	
	1000 The Chinese perfect gunpowder and begin to use it in warfare.
1500–1600 Region is under Portuguese control.	**1530** Beginning of transatlantic slave trade organized by the Portuguese in Africa.
	1558–1603 Reign of Elizabeth I of England
	1620 Pilgrims sail the *Mayflower* to America.
1760 Al-Khalifa and Al-Jalahimah clans arrive.	**1776** U.S. Declaration of Independence
1783 The clans capture Bahrain.	
1809 The two clans have control of the entire area.	**1789–99** The French Revolution
1816 Rahmah bin Jabir is ousted.	**1861** The U.S. Civil War begins.
	1869 The Suez Canal is opened.
	1914 World War I begins.
1930s Collapse of the pearl industry.	
1939 Natural oil and gas are discovered in Qatar.	**1939** World War II begins.
	1945 The United States drops atomic bombs on Hiroshima and Nagasaki.

IN QATAR	IN THE WORLD
1949 Oil production begins. **1960** Ahman ibd Ali takes over. **1964** Offshore oil production begins.	**1949** The North Atlantic Treaty Organization (NATO) is formed. **1966** The Chinese Cultural Revolution
1971 Qatar declares independence; North Field is discovered. **1973** Qatar begins using their own currency.	
	1986 Nuclear power disaster at Chernobyl in Ukraine **1991** Breakup of the Soviet Union
1996 Television station Al-Jazeera starts. **1999** First popular elections are held.	**1997** Hong Kong is returned to China.
2002 Constitution is drafted; United States tranfers military headquarters from Saudi Arabia; Qatar Tourism Authority is formed; e-government is launched.	**2001** Terrorists crash planes in New York, Washington, D.C., and Pennsylvania.
2003 Qatar acts as critical command center for the United States during the invasion of Iraq; President George Bush visits; the emir visits the United States; "Rashid the Recycler" program is launched. **2005** Constitution comes into force. **2006** Qatar hosts the Asian Games.	**2003** War in Iraq begins.

GLOSSARY

abayas
Islamic woman's long black silk dress

Acida
Bedouin dessert

al-sharq al-awsat
Arabic term for the Middle East

Ayyalah (aye-YAH-la)
Traditional Islamic dance with poetry and swords

Bedouin
Desert dweller

burkha (BUHR-kah)
A woman's veil

desalination
Removing the salt from ocean water

Eid al-Fitr
The festival of breaking the fast

expatriate
Somebody who has moved to another land to live or work

gutra
Head covering

hadith (heh-DEETH)
Collection of Islamic sayings

hajj
The pilgrimage to Mecca

henna
Dye made from the henna plant

hijra (HID-rah)
Mohammad's migration with his followers

majilis
A men's-only room for socializing

megnas
A hunting journey, usually with falcons

muezzin (my-EH-zin)
A religious caller to prayer who sings the call.

qahwa helw
Sweet, strong coffee

saum (sah-OOM)
Period of fasting

shahadah (sha-ha-DAH)
The declaration of Islamic faith

souq (SOOK)
Local market

wahhabis
Conservative Muslims

zakat (zah-KAHT)
The practice of giving to the poor

FURTHER INFORMATION

BOOKS

McCoy, Lisa. *Qatar*. Broomall, PA: Mason Crest Publishing, 2002.

Willis, Terri. *Qatar*. Danbury, CT: Children's Press, 2004.

WEB SITES

The CIA World Factbook. www.cia.gov/cia/publications/factbook/geos/qa.html

Qatar Information. www.qatar-info.com

Explore Qatar. www.exploreqatar.com

BIBLIOGRAPHY

Department of Foreign Affairs. *Qatar.* Qatar: Department of Information and Research, 2006.
Jones, Matthew. *Berlitz Pocket Guide to Qatar.* Singapore: Apa Publications, 2006.
Willis, Terri. Qatar. Danbury, CT: Children's Press, 2004.
Arab.net. www.arab.net
15th Asain Games–Doha 2006. www.doha-2006.com
Gulf Times. www.gulf-times.com
Qatarinfo.net. http://English.qatarinfo.net
Qatar National Olympic Committee. www.qatarolympics.org
Royal Embassy of Saudi Arabia. www.saudiembassy.net
United Nations Educational, Scientific, and Cultural Organization. http://portal.unesco.org
Welcome to Qatar. www.qatarembassy.net

INDEX